SSAT MIDDLE LEVEL MATH FOR BEGINNERS

The Ultimate Step by Step Guide to Preparing for the SSAT Middle Level Math Test

By

Reza Nazari

About Effortless Math Education

Effortless Math Education operates the www.effortlessmath.com website, which prepares and publishes Test prep and Mathematics learning resources. Effortless Math authors' team strives to prepare and publish the best quality Mathematics learning resources to make learning Math easier for all. We Help Students Learn to Love Mathematics.

All inquiries should be addressed to:
info@effortlessMath.com
www.EffortlessMath.com

ISBN: 978-1-63719-216-0

Published by: **Effortless Math Education Inc**

for Online Math Practice Visit www.EffortlessMath.com

Welcome to
SSAT Middle Level Math Prep 2023

Thank you for choosing Effortless Math for your SSAT Middle Level Math test preparation and congratulations on making the decision to take the SSAT Middle Level test! It's a remarkable move you are taking, one that shouldn't be diminished in any capacity. That's why you need to use every tool possible to ensure you succeed on the test with the highest possible score, and this extensive study guide is one such tool.

If math has never been a strong subject for you, **don't worry**! This book will help you prepare for (and even ACE) the SSAT Middle Level test's math section. As test day draws nearer, effective preparation becomes increasingly more important. Thankfully, you have this comprehensive study guide to help you get ready for the test. With this guide, you can feel confident that you will be more than ready for the SSAT Middle Level Math test when the time comes.

First and foremost, it is important to note that this book is a study guide and not a textbook. It is best read from cover to cover. Every lesson of this "self-guided math book" was carefully developed to ensure that you are making the most effective use of your time while preparing for the test. This up-to-date guide reflects the 2023 test guidelines and will put you on the right track to hone your math skills, overcome exam anxiety, and boost your confidence, so that you can have your best to succeed on the SSAT Middle Level Math test.

This study guide will:

☑ Explain the format of the SSAT Middle Level Math test.

☑ Describe specific test-taking strategies that you can use on the test.

☑ Provide SSAT Middle Level Math test-taking tips.

☑ Review all SSAT Middle Level Math concepts and topics you will be tested on.

☑ Help you identify the areas in which you need to concentrate your study time.

☑ Offer exercises that help you develop the basic math skills you will learn in each section.

☑ Give **2 realistic and full-length practice tests** (featuring new question types) with detailed answers to help you measure your exam readiness and build confidence.

This resource contains everything you will ever need to succeed on the SSAT Middle Level Math test. You'll get in-depth instructions on every math topic as well as tips and techniques on how to answer each question type. You'll also get plenty of practice questions to boost your test-taking confidence.

In addition, in the following pages you'll find:

➢ **How to Use This Book Effectively** – This section provides you with step-by-step instructions on how to get the most out of this comprehensive study guide.

➢ **How to study for the SSAT Middle Level Math Test** – A six-step study program has been developed to help you make the best use of this book and prepare for your SSAT

Middle Level Math test. Here you'll find tips and strategies to guide your study program and help you understand SSAT Middle Level Math and how to ace the test.

➢ **SSAT Middle Level Math Review** – Learn everything you need to know about the SSAT Middle Level Math test.

➢ **SSAT Middle Level Math Test-Taking Strategies** – Learn how to effectively put these recommended test-taking techniques into use for improving your SSAT Middle Level Math score.

➢ **Test Day Tips** – Review these tips to make sure you will do your best when the big day comes.

Effortless Math's SSAT Middle Level Online Center

Effortless Math Online SSAT Middle Level Center offers a complete study program, including the following:

✓ Step-by-step instructions on how to prepare for the SSAT Math test

✓ Numerous SSAT Math worksheets to help you measure your math skills

✓ Complete list of SSAT Math formulas

✓ Video lessons for all SSAT Math topics

✓ Full-length SSAT Math practice tests

✓ And much more…

No Registration Required.

Visit effortlessmath.com/SSATMiddle to find your online SSAT Middle Level Math resources.

How to Use This Book Effectively

Look no further when you need a study guide to improve your math skills to succeed on the math portion of the SSAT Middle Level test. Each chapter of this comprehensive guide to the SSAT Middle Level Math will provide you with the knowledge, tools, and understanding needed for every topic covered on the test.

It's imperative that you understand each topic before moving onto another one, as that's the way to guarantee your success. Each topic provides you with examples and a step-by-step guide of every concept to better understand the content that will be on the test. To get the best possible results from this book:

> **Begin studying long before your test date**. This provides you ample time to learn the different math concepts. The earlier you begin studying for the test, the sharper your skills will be. Do not procrastinate! Provide yourself with plenty of time to learn the concepts and feel comfortable that you understand them when your test date arrives.

> **Practice consistently**. Study SSAT Middle Level Math concepts at least 20 to 30 minutes a day. Remember, slow and steady wins the race, which can be applied to preparing for the SSAT Middle Level Math test. Instead of cramming to tackle everything at once, be patient and learn the math topics in short bursts.

> Whenever you get a math problem wrong, **mark it off, and review it later** to make sure you understand the concept.

> Start each session by **looking over the previous material.**

> Once you've reviewed the book's lessons, **take the practice test at the back of the book** to gauge your level of readiness. Then, review your results. Read detailed answers and solutions for each question you missed.

> **Take another practice test** to get an idea of how ready you are to take the actual exam. Taking the practice tests will give you the confidence you need on test day. Simulate the SSAT Middle Level testing environment by sitting in a quiet room free from distraction. Make sure to clock yourself with a timer.

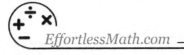

How to Study for the SSAT Middle Level Math Test

Studying for the SSAT Middle Level Math test can be a really daunting and boring task. What's the best way to go about it? Is there a certain study method that works better than others? Well, studying for the SSAT Middle Level Math can be done effectively. The following six-step program has been designed to make preparing for the SSAT Middle Level Math test more efficient and less overwhelming.

Step 1 - Create a study plan
Step 2 - Choose your study resources
Step 3 - Review, Learn, Practice
Step 4 - Learn and practice test-taking strategies
Step 5 - Learn the SSAT Middle Level Test format and take practice tests
Step 6 - Analyze your performance

STEP 1: Create a Study Plan

It's always easier to get things done when you have a plan. Creating a study plan for the SSAT Middle Level Math test can help you to stay on track with your studies. It's important to sit down and prepare a study plan with what works with your life, school, and any other obligations you may have. Devote enough time each day to studying. It's also a great idea to break down each section of the exam into blocks and study one concept at a time.

It's important to understand that there is no "right" way to create a study plan. Your study plan will be personalized based on your specific needs and learning style.

Follow these guidelines to create an effective study plan for your SSAT Middle Level Math test:

★ **Analyze your learning style and study habits** – Everyone has a different learning style. It is essential to embrace your individuality and the unique way you learn. Think about what works and what doesn't work for you. Do you prefer SSAT Middle Level Math prep books or a combination of textbooks and video lessons? Does it work better for you if you study every night for thirty minutes or is it more effective to study in the morning before going to school?

★ **Evaluate your schedule** – Review your current schedule and find out how much time you can consistently devote to SSAT Math study.

★ **Develop a schedule** – Now it's time to add your study schedule to your calendar like any other obligation. Schedule time for study, practice, and review. Plan out which topic you will study on which day to ensure that you're devoting enough time to each concept. Develop a study plan that is mindful, realistic, and flexible.

★ **Stick to your schedule** – A study plan is only effective when it is followed consistently. You should try to develop a study plan that you can follow for the length of your study program.

★ **Evaluate your study plan and adjust as needed** – Sometimes you need to adjust your plan when you have new commitments. Check in with yourself regularly to make sure that you're not falling behind in your study plan. Remember, the most important thing is sticking to your plan. Your study plan is all about helping you be more productive. If you find that your study plan is not as effective as you want, don't get discouraged. It's okay to make changes as you figure out what works best for you.

STEP 2: Choose Your Study Resources

There are numerous textbooks and online resources available for the SSAT Middle Level Math test, and it may not be clear where to begin. Don't worry! This study guide provides everything you need to fully prepare for your SSAT Middle Level Math test. In addition to the book content, you can also use Effortless Math's online resources. (video lessons, worksheets, formulas, etc.) On each page, there is a link (and a QR code) to an online webpage which provides a comprehensive review of the topic, step-by-step instruction, video tutorial, and numerous examples and exercises to help you fully understand the concept.

You can also visit EffortlessMath.com/SSATMiddle to find your online SSAT Middle Level Math resources.

STEP 3: Review, Learn, Practice

This SSAT Middle Level Math study guide breaks down each subject into specific skills or content areas. For instance, the percent concept is separated into different topics–percent calculation, percent increase and decrease, percent problems, etc. Use this study guide and Effortless Math online SSAT Middle Level center to help you go over all key math concepts and topics on the SSAT Middle Level Math test.

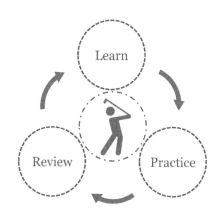

As you read each topic, take notes or highlight the concepts you would like to go over again in the future. If you're unfamiliar with a topic or something is difficult for you, use the link (or the QR code) at the bottom of the page to find the webpage that provides more instruction about that topic. For each math topic, plenty of instructions, step-by-step guides, and examples are provided to ensure you get a good grasp of the material.

Quickly review the topics you do understand to get a brush-up of the material. Be sure to do the practice questions provided at the end of every chapter to measure your understanding of the concepts.

STEP 4: Learn and Practice Test-taking Strategies

In the following sections, you will find important test-taking strategies and tips that can help you earn extra points. You'll learn how to think strategically and when to guess if you don't know the answer to a question. Using SSAT Middle Level Math test-taking strategies and tips can help you raise your score and do well on the test. Apply test taking strategies on the practice tests to help you boost your confidence.

STEP 5: Learn the SSAT Middle Level Test Format and Take Practice Tests

The SSAT Middle Level *Test Review* section provides information about the structure of the SSAT Middle Level test. Read this section to learn more about the SSAT Middle Level test structure, different test sections, the number of questions in each section, and the section time limits. When you have a prior understanding of the test format and different types of SSAT Middle Level Math questions, you'll feel more confident when you take the actual exam.

Once you have read through the instructions and lessons and feel like you are ready to go – take advantage of both of the full-length SSAT Middle Level Math practice tests available in this study guide. Use the practice tests to sharpen your skills and build confidence.

The SSAT Middle Level Math practice tests offered at the end of the book are formatted similarly to the actual SSAT Middle Level Math test. When you take each practice test, try to simulate actual testing conditions. To take the practice tests, sit in a quiet space, time yourself, and work through as many of the questions as time allows. The practice tests are followed by detailed answer explanations to help you find your weak areas, learn from your mistakes, and raise your SSAT Middle Level Math score.

STEP 6: Analyze Your Performance

After taking the practice tests, look over the answer keys and explanations to learn which questions you answered correctly and which you did not. Never be discouraged if you make a few mistakes. See them as a learning opportunity. This will highlight your strengths and weaknesses.

You can use the results to determine if you need additional practice or if you are ready to take the actual SSAT Middle Level Math test.

Looking for more?

Visit effortlessmath.com/SSATMiddle to find hundreds of SSAT Middle Level Math worksheets, video tutorials, practice tests, SSAT Middle Level Math formulas, and much more.

Or scan this QR code.

No Registration Required.

SSAT Middle Level Test Review

The SSAT, or Secondary School Admissions Test, is a standardized test to help determine admission to private elementary, middle and high schools.

There are currently three Levels of the SSAT:

- ✓ Lower Level (for students in 3rd and 4th grade)

- ✓ Middle Level (for students in 5th-7th grade)

- ✓ Upper Level (for students in 8th-11th grade)

There are six sections on the SSAT Middle Level Test:

- ✓ Writing: 25 minutes.

- ✓ Math section: 25 questions, 30 minutes

- ✓ Reading section: 40 questions, 40 minutes

- ✓ Verbal section: 60 questions, 30 minutes

- ✓ Math section: 25 questions, 30 minutes

- ✓ Experimental: 16 questions, 15 minutes.

The SSAT Middle-Level Math test has two sections. Each section contains 25 questions and test takers are given 30 minutes to complete the test. This test measures the ability of test-takers to solve problems related to elementary algebra, arithmetic, geometry, and other concepts.

Students are not allowed to use a calculator in the SSAT Middle-Level Math Test. In this test, test takers receive 1 point for each correct answer, and they lose ¼ point for each wrong one. For unanswered questions, test-takers receive 0 points.

SSAT Middle Level Math Test-Taking Strategies

Here are some test-taking strategies that you can use to maximize your performance and results on the SSAT Middle Level Math test.

#1: USE THIS APPROACH TO ANSWER EVERY SSAT MIDDLE LEVEL MATH QUESTION

- Review the question to identify keywords and important information.

- Translate the keywords into math operations so you can solve the problem.

- Review the answer choices. What are the differences between answer choices?

- Draw or label a diagram if needed.

- Try to find patterns.

- Find the right method to answer the question. Use straightforward math, plug in numbers, or test the answer choices (backsolving).

- Double-check your work.

#2: USE EDUCATED GUESSING

This approach is applicable to the problems you understand to some degree but cannot solve using straightforward math. In such cases, try to filter out as many answer choices as possible before picking an answer. In cases where you don't have a clue about what a certain problem entails, don't waste any time trying to eliminate answer choices. Just choose one randomly before moving onto the next question.

As you can ascertain, direct solutions are the most optimal approach. Carefully read through the question, determine what the solution is using the math you have learned before, then coordinate the answer with one of the choices available to you. Are you stumped? Make your best guess, then move on.

Don't leave any fields empty! Even if you're unable to work out a problem, strive to answer it. Take a guess if you have to. You will not lose points by getting an answer wrong, though you may gain a point by getting it correct!

#3 : BALLPARK

A ballpark answer is a rough approximation. When we become overwhelmed by calculations and figures, we end up making silly mistakes. A decimal that is moved by one unit can change an answer from right to wrong, regardless of the number of steps that you went through to get it. That's where ballparking can play a big part.

If you think you know what the correct answer may be (even if it's just a ballpark answer), you'll usually have the ability to eliminate a couple of choices. While answer choices are usually based on the average student error and/or values that are closely tied, you will still be able to weed out choices that are way far afield. Try to find answers that aren't in the proverbial ballpark when you're looking for a wrong answer on a multiple-choice question. This is an optimal approach to eliminating answers to a problem.

#4 : BACKSOLVING

All questions on the SSAT Middle Level Math test will be in multiple-choice format. Many test-takers prefer multiple-choice questions, as at least the answer is right there. You'll typically have five answers to pick from. You simply need to figure out which one is correct. Usually, the best way to go about doing so is "backsolving."

As mentioned earlier, direct solutions are the most optimal approach to answering a question. Carefully read through a problem, calculate a solution, then correspond the answer with one of the choices displayed in front of you. If you can't calculate a solution, your next best approach involves "backsolving."

When backsolving a problem, contrast one of your answer options against the problem you are asked, then see which of them is most relevant. More often than not, answer choices are listed in ascending or descending order. In such cases, try out the choices B or C. If it's not correct, you can go either down or up from there.

#5 : PLUGGING IN NUMBERS

"Plugging in numbers" is a strategy that can be applied to a wide range of different math problems on the SSAT Middle Level Math test. This approach is typically used to simplify a challenging question so that it is more understandable. By using the strategy carefully, you can find the answer without too much trouble.

The concept is fairly straightforward–replace unknown variables in a problem with certain values. When selecting a number, consider the following:

- Choose a number that's basic (just not too basic). Generally, you should avoid choosing 1 (or even 0). A decent choice is 2.

- Try not to choose a number that is displayed in the problem.

- Make sure you keep your numbers different if you need to choose at least two of them.

- More often than not, choosing numbers merely lets you filter out some of your answer choices. As such, don't just go with the first choice that gives you the right answer.

- If several answers seem correct, then you'll need to choose another value and try again. This time, though, you'll just need to check choices that haven't been eliminated yet.

- If your question contains fractions, then a potential right answer may involve either an LCD (least common denominator) or an LCD multiple.

- 100 is the number you should choose when you are dealing with problems involving percentages.

SSAT Middle Level Math – Test Day Tips

After practicing and reviewing all the math concepts you've been taught, and taking some SSAT Middle Level mathematics practice tests, you'll be prepared for test day. Consider the following tips to be extra-ready come test time.

Before Your Test

What to do the night before:

■ **Relax!** One day before your test, study lightly or skip studying altogether. You shouldn't attempt to learn something new, either. There are plenty of reasons why studying the evening before a big test can work against you. Put it this way–a marathoner wouldn't go out for a sprint before the day of a big race. Mental marathoners–such as yourself–should not study for any more than one hour 24 hours before a SSAT Middle Level test. That's because your brain requires some rest to be at its best. The night before your exam, spend some time with family or friends, or read a book.

■ **Avoid bright screens** - You'll have to get some good shuteye the night before your test. Bright screens (such as the ones coming from your laptop, TV, or mobile device) should be avoided altogether. Staring at such a screen will keep your brain up, making it hard to drift asleep at a reasonable hour.

■ **Make sure your dinner is healthy** - The meal that you have for dinner should be nutritious. Be sure to drink plenty of water as well. Load up on your complex carbohydrates, much like a marathon runner would do. Pasta, rice, and potatoes are ideal options here, as are vegetables and protein sources.

■ **Get your bag ready for test day** - The night prior to your test, pack your bag with your stationery, admissions pass, ID, and any other gear that you need. Keep the bag right by your front door.

■ **Make plans to reach the testing site** - Before going to sleep, ensure that you understand precisely how you will arrive at the site of the test. If parking is something you'll have to find first, plan for it. If you're dependent on public transit, then review the schedule. You should also make sure that the train/bus/subway/streetcar you use will be running. Find out about road closures as well. If a parent or friend is accompanying you, ensure that they understand what steps they have to take as well.

The Day of the Test

- **Get up reasonably early, but not too early.**

- **Have breakfast** - Breakfast improves your concentration, memory, and mood. As such, make sure the breakfast that you eat in the morning is healthy. The last thing you want to be is distracted by a grumbling tummy. If it's not your own stomach making those noises, another test taker close to you might be instead. Prevent discomfort or embarrassment by consuming a healthy breakfast. Bring a snack with you if you think you'll need it.

- **Follow your daily routine** - Do you watch TV each morning while getting ready for the day? Don't break your usual habits on the day of the test. Likewise, if coffee isn't something you drink in the morning, then don't take up the habit hours before your test. Routine consistency lets you concentrate on the main objective—doing the best you can on your test.

- **Wear layers** - Dress yourself up in comfortable layers. You should be ready for any kind of internal temperature. If it gets too warm during the test, take a layer off.

- **Get there on time** - The last thing you want to do is get to the test site late. Rather, you should be there 45 minutes prior to the start of the test. Upon your arrival, try not to hang out with anybody who is nervous. Any anxious energy they exhibit shouldn't influence you.

- **Leave the books at home** - No books should be brought to the test site. If you start developing anxiety before the test, books could encourage you to do some last-minute studying, which will only hinder you. Keep the books far away–better yet, leave them at home.

- **Make your voice heard** - If something is off, speak to a proctor. If medical attention is needed or if you'll require anything, consult the proctor prior to the start of the test. Any doubts you have should be clarified. You should be entering the test site with a state of mind that is completely clear.

- **Have faith in yourself** - When you feel confident, you will be able to perform at your best. When you are waiting for the test to begin, envision yourself receiving an outstanding result. Try to see yourself as someone who knows all the answers, no matter what the questions are. A lot of athletes tend to use this technique–particularly before a big competition. Your expectations will be reflected by your performance.

During your test

- **Be calm and breathe deeply** - You need to relax before the test, and some deep breathing will go a long way to help you do that. Be confident and calm. You got this. Everybody feels a little stressed out just before an evaluation of any kind is set to begin. Learn some effective breathing exercises. Spend a minute meditating before the test starts. Filter out any negative thoughts you have. Exhibit confidence when having such thoughts.

- **Concentrate on the test** - Refrain from comparing yourself to anyone else. You shouldn't be distracted by the people near you or random noise. Concentrate exclusively on the test. If you find yourself irritated by surrounding noises, earplugs can be used to block sounds off close to you. Don't forget–the test is going to last several hours if you're taking more than one subject of the test. Some of that time will be dedicated to brief sections. Concentrate on the specific section you are working on during a particular moment. Do not let your mind wander off to upcoming or previous sections.

- **Skip challenging questions** - Optimize your time when taking the test. Lingering on a single question for too long will work against you. If you don't know what the answer is to a certain question, use your best guess, and mark the question so you can review it later on. There is no need to spend time attempting to solve something you aren't sure about. That time would be better served handling the questions you can actually answer well. You will not be penalized for getting the wrong answer on a test like this.

- **Try to answer each question individually** - Focus only on the question you are working on. Use one of the test-taking strategies to solve the problem. If you aren't able to come up with an answer, don't get frustrated. Simply skip that question, then move onto the next one.

- **Don't forget to breathe!** Whenever you notice your mind wandering, your stress levels boosting, or frustration brewing, take a thirty-second break. Shut your eyes, drop your pencil, breathe deeply, and let your shoulders relax. You will end up being more productive when you allow yourself to relax for a moment.

- **Review your answer.** If you still have time at the end of the test, don't waste it. Go back and check over your answers. It is worth going through the test from start to finish to ensure that you didn't make a sloppy mistake somewhere.

- **Optimize your breaks** - When break time comes, use the restroom, have a snack, and reactivate your energy for the subsequent section. Doing some stretches can help stimulate your blood flow.

After your test

- **Take it easy** - You will need to set some time aside to relax and decompress once the test has concluded. There is no need to stress yourself out about what you could've said, or what you may have done wrong. At this point, there's nothing you can do about it. Your energy and time would be better spent on something that will bring you happiness for the remainder of your day.

■ **Redoing the test** - Did you pass the test? Congratulations! Your hard work paid off!

If you have failed your test, though, don't worry! The test can be retaken. In such cases, you will need to follow the retake policy. You also need to re-register to take the exam again.

Contents

CHAPTER: **Statistics**   **89**

CHAPTER

1 Fractions and Mixed Numbers

Math topics that you'll learn in this chapter:

☑ Simplifying Fractions

☑ Adding and Subtracting Fractions

☑ Multiplying and Dividing Fractions

☑ Adding Mixed Numbers

☑ Subtracting Mixed Numbers

☑ Multiplying Mixed Numbers

☑ Dividing Mixed Numbers

1

Simplifying Fractions

- A fraction contains two numbers separated by a bar between them. The bottom number, called the denominator, is the total number of equally divided portions in one whole. The top number, called the numerator, is how many portions you have. And the bar represents the operation of division.

- Simplifying a fraction means reducing it to the lowest terms. To simplify a fraction, evenly divide both the top and bottom of the fraction by $2, 3, 5, 7$, etc.

- Continue until you can't go any further.

Examples:

Example 1. Simplify $\frac{18}{30}$

Solution: To simplify $\frac{18}{30}$, find a number that both 18 and 30 are divisible by. Both are divisible by 6. Then: $\frac{18}{30} = \frac{18 \div 6}{30 \div 6} = \frac{3}{5}$

Example 2. Simplify $\frac{48}{80}$

Solution: To simplify $\frac{48}{80}$, find a number that both 48 and 80 are divisible by. Both are divisible by 8 and 16. Then: $\frac{48}{80} = \frac{48 \div 8}{80 \div 8} = \frac{6}{10}$, 6 and 10 are divisible by 2, then: $\frac{6}{10} = \frac{3}{5}$ or $\frac{48}{80} = \frac{48 \div 16}{80 \div 16} = \frac{3}{5}$

Example 3. Simplify $\frac{40}{120}$

Solution: To simplify $\frac{40}{120}$, find a number that both 40 and 120 are divisible by. Both are divisible by 40, then: $\frac{40}{120} = \frac{40 \div 40}{120 \div 40} = \frac{1}{3}$

Adding and Subtracting Fractions

- For "like" fractions (fractions with the same denominator), add or subtract the numerators (top numbers) and write the answer over the common denominator (bottom numbers).

- Adding and Subtracting fractions with the same denominator:

- $$\frac{a}{b} + \frac{c}{b} = \frac{a+c}{b} \qquad \frac{a}{b} - \frac{c}{b} = \frac{a-c}{b}$$

- Find equivalent fractions with the same denominator before you can add or subtract fractions with different denominators.

- Adding and Subtracting fractions with different denominators:

$$\frac{a}{b} + \frac{c}{d} = \frac{ad+bc}{bd} \qquad \frac{a}{b} - \frac{c}{d} = \frac{ad-bc}{bd}$$

Examples:

Example 4. Find the sum. $\frac{2}{3} + \frac{1}{2} =$

Solution: These two fractions are "unlike" fractions. (they have different denominators). Use this formula: $\frac{a}{b} + \frac{c}{d} = \frac{ad+cb}{bd}$

Then: $\frac{2}{3} + \frac{1}{2} = \frac{(2)(2)+(3)(1)}{3\times 2} = \frac{4+3}{6} = \frac{7}{6}$

Example 5. Find the difference. $\frac{3}{5} - \frac{2}{7} =$

Solution: For "unlike" fractions, find equivalent fractions with the same denominator before you can add or subtract fractions with different denominators. Use this formula:

$\frac{a}{b} - \frac{c}{d} = \frac{ad-bc}{bd}$

$\frac{3}{5} - \frac{2}{7} = \frac{(3)(7)-(2)(5)}{5\times 7} = \frac{21-10}{35} = \frac{11}{35}$

bit.ly/3x5jfwe

Find more at

Multiplying and Dividing Fractions

- Multiplying fractions: multiply the top numbers and multiply the bottom numbers. Simplify if necessary. $\frac{a}{b} \times \frac{c}{d} = \frac{a \times c}{b \times d}$

- Dividing fractions: Keep, Change, Flip

- Keep the first fraction, change the division sign to multiplication, and flip the numerator and denominator of the second fraction. Then, solve!

$$\frac{a}{b} \div \frac{c}{d} = \frac{a}{b} \times \frac{d}{c} = \frac{a \times d}{b \times c}$$

Examples:

Example 1. Multiply. $\frac{2}{3} \times \frac{3}{5} =$

Solution: Multiply the top numbers and multiply the bottom numbers.
$\frac{2}{3} \times \frac{3}{5} = \frac{2 \times 3}{3 \times 5} = \frac{6}{15}$

Example 2. Solve. $\frac{3}{4} \div \frac{2}{5} =$

Solution: Keep the first fraction, change the division sign to multiplication, and flip the numerator and denominator of the second fraction.
Then: $\frac{3}{4} \div \frac{2}{5} = \frac{3}{4} \times \frac{5}{2} = \frac{3 \times 5}{4 \times 2} = \frac{15}{8}$

Example 3. Calculate. $\frac{4}{5} \times \frac{3}{4} =$

Solution: Multiply the top numbers and multiply the bottom numbers.
$\frac{4}{5} \times \frac{3}{4} = \frac{4 \times 3}{5 \times 4} = \frac{12}{20}$, simplify: $\frac{12}{20} = \frac{12 \div 4}{20 \div 4} = \frac{3}{5}$

Example 4. Solve. $\frac{5}{6} \div \frac{3}{7} =$

Solution: Keep the first fraction, change the division sign to multiplication, and flip the numerator and denominator of the second fraction.
Then: $\frac{5}{6} \div \frac{3}{7} = \frac{5}{6} \times \frac{7}{3} = \frac{5 \times 7}{6 \times 3} = \frac{35}{18}$

Adding Mixed Numbers

Use the following steps for adding mixed numbers:

- Add whole numbers of the mixed numbers.

- Add the fractions of the mixed numbers.

- Find the Least Common Denominator (LCD) if necessary.

- Add whole numbers and fractions.

- Write your answer in lowest terms.

Examples:

Example 1. Add mixed numbers. $2\frac{1}{2} + 1\frac{2}{3} =$

Solution: Let's rewriting our equation with parts separated, $2\frac{1}{2} + 1\frac{2}{3} = 2 + \frac{1}{2} + 1 + \frac{2}{3}$. Now, add whole number parts: $2 + 1 = 3$

Add the fraction parts $\frac{1}{2} + \frac{2}{3}$. Rewrite to solve with the equivalent fractions. $\frac{1}{2} + \frac{2}{3} = \frac{3}{6} + \frac{4}{6} = \frac{7}{6}$. The answer is an improper fraction (numerator is bigger than denominator). Convert the improper fraction into a mixed number: $\frac{7}{6} = 1\frac{1}{6}$. Now, combine the whole and fraction parts: $3 + 1\frac{1}{6} = 4\frac{1}{6}$

Example 2. Find the sum. $1\frac{3}{4} + 2\frac{1}{2} =$

Solution: Rewriting our equation with parts separated, $1 + \frac{3}{4} + 2 + \frac{1}{2}$. Add the whole number parts:

$1 + 2 = 3$. Add the fraction parts: $\frac{3}{4} + \frac{1}{2} = \frac{3}{4} + \frac{2}{4} = \frac{5}{4}$

Convert the improper fraction into a mixed number: $\frac{5}{4} = 1\frac{1}{4}$.

Now, combine the whole and fraction parts: $3 + 1\frac{1}{4} = 4\frac{1}{4}$

bit.ly/2M4oABB

Find more at

Subtract Mixed Numbers

Use these steps for subtracting mixed numbers.

- Convert mixed numbers into improper fractions. $a\frac{c}{b} = \frac{ab+c}{b}$

- Find equivalent fractions with the same denominator for unlike fractions. (fractions with different denominators)

- Subtract the second fraction from the first one. $\frac{a}{b} - \frac{c}{d} = \frac{ad-bc}{bd}$

- Write your answer in lowest terms.

- If the answer is an improper fraction, convert it into a mixed number.

Examples:

Example 1. Subtract. $2\frac{1}{3} - 1\frac{1}{2} =$

Solution: Convert mixed numbers into fractions: $2\frac{1}{3} = \frac{2\times3+1}{3} = \frac{7}{3}$ and $1\frac{1}{2} = \frac{1\times2+1}{2} = \frac{3}{2}$

These two fractions are "unlike" fractions. (they have different denominators). Find equivalent fractions with the same denominator. Use this formula: $\frac{a}{b} - \frac{c}{d} = \frac{ad-bc}{bd}$

$$\frac{7}{3} - \frac{3}{2} = \frac{(7)(2)-(3)(3)}{3\times2} = \frac{14-9}{6} = \frac{5}{6}$$

Example 2. Subtract. $3\frac{4}{7} - 2\frac{3}{4} =$

Solution: Convert mixed numbers into fractions: $3\frac{4}{7} = \frac{3\times7+4}{7} = \frac{25}{7}$ and $2\frac{3}{4} = \frac{2\times4+3}{4} = \frac{11}{4}$

Then: $3\frac{4}{7} - 2\frac{3}{4} = \frac{25}{7} - \frac{11}{4} = \frac{(25)(4)-(11)(7)}{7\times4} = \frac{23}{28}$

Multiplying Mixed Numbers

Use the following steps for multiplying mixed numbers:

- Convert the mixed numbers into fractions. $a\frac{c}{b} = a + \frac{c}{b} = \frac{ab+c}{b}$

- Multiply fractions. $\frac{a}{b} \times \frac{c}{d} = \frac{a \times c}{b \times d}$

- Write your answer in lowest terms.

- If the answer is an improper fraction (numerator is bigger than denominator), convert it into a mixed number.

Examples:

Example 1. Multiply. $4\frac{1}{2} \times 2\frac{2}{5} =$

Solution: Convert mixed numbers into fractions, $4\frac{1}{2} = \frac{4 \times 2 + 1}{2} = \frac{9}{2}$ and
$$2\frac{2}{5} = \frac{2 \times 5 + 2}{5} = \frac{12}{5}$$
Apply the fractions rule for multiplication, $\frac{9}{2} \times \frac{12}{5} = \frac{9 \times 12}{2 \times 5} = \frac{108}{10}$
The answer is an improper fraction. Convert it into a mixed number. $\frac{108}{10} = 10\frac{4}{5}$

Example 2. Multiply. $3\frac{2}{3} \times 2\frac{5}{6} =$

Solution: Converting mixed numbers into fractions, $3\frac{2}{3} \times 2\frac{5}{6} = \frac{11}{3} \times \frac{17}{6}$
Apply the fractions rule for multiplication, $\frac{11}{3} \times \frac{17}{6} = \frac{11 \times 17}{3 \times 6} = \frac{187}{18} = 10\frac{7}{18}$

Example 3. Multiply mixed numbers. $5\frac{1}{4} \times 3\frac{3}{8} =$

Solution: Converting mixed numbers to fractions, $5\frac{1}{4} = \frac{21}{4}$ and $3\frac{3}{8} = \frac{27}{8}$. Multiply

two fractions:

$\frac{21}{4} \times \frac{27}{8} = \frac{21 \times 27}{4 \times 8} = \frac{567}{32} = 17\frac{23}{32}$

bit.ly/3aPy7XJ

Find more at

Dividing Mixed Numbers

Use the following steps for dividing mixed numbers:

- Convert the mixed numbers into fractions. $a\frac{c}{b} = a + \frac{c}{b} = \frac{ab+c}{b}$

- Divide fractions: Keep, Change, Flip: Keep the first fraction, change the division sign to multiplication, and flip the numerator and denominator of the second fraction. Then, solve! $\frac{a}{b} \div \frac{c}{d} = \frac{a}{b} \times \frac{d}{c} = \frac{a \times d}{b \times c}$

- Write your answer in lowest terms.

- If the answer is an improper fraction (numerator is bigger than denominator), convert it into a mixed number.

Examples:

Example 1. Solve. $2\frac{1}{3} \div 1\frac{1}{2}$

Solution: Convert mixed numbers into fractions: $2\frac{1}{3} = \frac{2 \times 3 + 1}{3} = \frac{7}{3}$ and $1\frac{1}{2} = \frac{1 \times 2 + 1}{2} = \frac{3}{2}$
Keep, Change, Flip: $\frac{7}{3} \div \frac{3}{2} = \frac{7}{3} \times \frac{2}{3} = \frac{7 \times 2}{3 \times 3} = \frac{14}{9}$. The answer is an improper fraction. Convert it into a mixed number: $\frac{14}{9} = 1\frac{5}{9}$

Example 2. Solve. $3\frac{3}{4} \div 2\frac{2}{5}$

Solution: Convert mixed numbers to fractions, then solve:
$3\frac{3}{4} \div 2\frac{2}{5} = \frac{15}{4} \div \frac{12}{5} = \frac{15}{4} \times \frac{5}{12} = \frac{75}{48} = 1\frac{9}{16}$

Example 3. Solve. $2\frac{4}{5} \div 1\frac{2}{3}$

Solution: Converting mixed numbers to fractions: $2\frac{4}{5} \div 1\frac{2}{3} = \frac{14}{5} \div \frac{5}{3}$
Keep, Change, Flip: $\frac{14}{5} \div \frac{5}{3} = \frac{14}{5} \times \frac{3}{5} = \frac{14 \times 3}{5 \times 5} = \frac{42}{25} = 1\frac{17}{25}$

Chapter 1: Practices

✍ Simplify each fraction.

1) $\dfrac{2}{8} =$

2) $\dfrac{5}{15} =$

3) $\dfrac{10}{90} =$

4) $\dfrac{12}{16} =$

5) $\dfrac{25}{45} =$

6) $\dfrac{42}{54} =$

7) $\dfrac{48}{60} =$

8) $\dfrac{52}{169} =$

✍ Find the sum or difference.

9) $\dfrac{3}{10} + \dfrac{2}{10} =$

10) $\dfrac{4}{9} - \dfrac{1}{9} =$

11) $\dfrac{2}{3} + \dfrac{6}{15} =$

12) $\dfrac{17}{24} - \dfrac{5}{8} =$

13) $\dfrac{7}{54} - \dfrac{1}{9} =$

14) $\dfrac{4}{5} - \dfrac{1}{6} =$

15) $\dfrac{6}{7} - \dfrac{3}{8} =$

16) $\dfrac{2}{13} + \dfrac{1}{4} =$

✍ Find the products or quotients.

17) $\dfrac{2}{9} \div \dfrac{4}{3} =$

18) $\dfrac{14}{5} \div \dfrac{28}{35} =$

19) $\dfrac{9}{25} \times \dfrac{5}{27} =$

20) $\dfrac{65}{72} \times \dfrac{12}{15} =$

✍ Find the sum.

21) $2\dfrac{1}{5} + 1\dfrac{2}{5} =$

22) $5\dfrac{1}{9} + 2\dfrac{7}{9} =$

23) $2\dfrac{3}{4} + 1\dfrac{1}{8} =$

24) $2\dfrac{2}{7} + 4\dfrac{1}{21} =$

25) $5\dfrac{3}{5} + 1\dfrac{4}{9} =$

26) $3\dfrac{3}{11} + 4\dfrac{6}{7} =$

Effortless
Math
Education

✎ **Find the difference**.

27) $5\frac{1}{3} - 4\frac{2}{3} =$

31) $4\frac{3}{4} - 2\frac{1}{28} =$

28) $4\frac{7}{10} - 1\frac{3}{10} =$

32) $4\frac{2}{7} - 3\frac{1}{6} =$

29) $3\frac{1}{3} - 2\frac{2}{9} =$

33) $5\frac{3}{10} - 3\frac{3}{4} =$

30) $6\frac{1}{2} - 3\frac{1}{3} =$

34) $6\frac{9}{20} - 2\frac{1}{3} =$

✎ **Find the products.**

35) $1\frac{1}{2} \times 2\frac{3}{7} =$

39) $2\frac{1}{5} \times 5\frac{1}{2} =$

36) $1\frac{3}{4} \times 1\frac{3}{5} =$

40) $2\frac{1}{2} \times 4\frac{4}{5} =$

37) $4\frac{1}{2} \times 1\frac{5}{6} =$

41) $3\frac{1}{5} \times 4\frac{1}{2} =$

38) $1\frac{2}{7} \times 3\frac{1}{5} =$

42) $4\frac{9}{10} \times 4\frac{1}{2} =$

✎ **Solve.**

43) $1\frac{1}{3} \div 1\frac{2}{3} =$

47) $4\frac{1}{5} \div 2\frac{2}{3} =$

44) $2\frac{1}{4} \div 1\frac{1}{2} =$

48) $1\frac{2}{3} \div 1\frac{3}{8} =$

45) $5\frac{1}{3} \div 3\frac{1}{2} =$

49) $4\frac{1}{2} \div 2\frac{2}{3} =$

46) $3\frac{2}{7} \div 1\frac{1}{8} =$

50) $1\frac{2}{11} \div 1\frac{1}{8} =$

Effortless
Math
Education

Chapter 1: Answers

1) $\frac{1}{4}$

2) $\frac{1}{3}$

3) $\frac{1}{9}$

4) $\frac{3}{4}$

5) $\frac{5}{9}$

6) $\frac{7}{9}$

7) $\frac{4}{5}$

8) $\frac{4}{13}$

9) $\frac{1}{2}$

10) $\frac{1}{3}$

11) $\frac{16}{15} = 1\frac{1}{15}$

12) $\frac{1}{12}$

13) $\frac{1}{54}$

14) $\frac{19}{30}$

15) $\frac{27}{56}$

16) $\frac{21}{52}$

17) $\frac{1}{6}$

18) $\frac{7}{2} = 3\frac{1}{2}$

19) $\frac{1}{15}$

20) $\frac{13}{18}$

21) $3\frac{3}{5}$

22) $7\frac{8}{9}$

23) $3\frac{7}{8}$

24) $6\frac{1}{3}$

25) $7\frac{2}{45}$

26) $8\frac{10}{77}$

27) $\frac{2}{3}$

28) $3\frac{2}{5}$

29) $1\frac{1}{9}$

30) $3\frac{1}{6}$

31) $2\frac{5}{7}$

32) $1\frac{5}{42}$

33) $1\frac{11}{20}$

34) $4\frac{7}{60}$

35) $3\frac{9}{14}$

36) $2\frac{4}{5}$

37) $8\frac{1}{4}$

38) $4\frac{4}{35}$

39) $12\frac{1}{10}$

40) 12

41) $14\frac{2}{5}$

42) $22\frac{1}{20}$

43) $\frac{4}{5}$

44) $1\frac{1}{2}$

45) $1\frac{11}{21}$

46) $2\frac{58}{63}$

47) $1\frac{23}{40}$

48) $1\frac{7}{33}$

49) $1\frac{11}{16}$

50) $1\frac{5}{99}$

Effortless Math Education

CHAPTER

2 Decimals

Math topics that you'll learn in this chapter:

☑ Comparing Decimals

☑ Rounding Decimals

☑ Adding and Subtracting Decimals

☑ Multiplying and Dividing Decimals

Comparing Decimals

- A decimal is a fraction written in a special form. For example, instead of writing $\frac{1}{2}$ you can write 0.5

- A Decimal Number contains a Decimal Point. It separates the whole number part from the fractional part of a decimal number.

- Let's review decimal place values: Example: 53.9861

5: tens	3: ones	9: tenths
8: hundredths	6: thousandths	1: tens thousandths

- To compare decimals, compare each digit of two decimals in the same place value. Start from left. Compare hundreds, tens, ones, tenth, hundredth, etc.

- To compare numbers, use these symbols:

Equal to =,	Less than <,	Greater than >
Greater than or equal ≥,	Less than or equal ≤	

Examples:

Example 1. Compare 0.03 and 0.30.

Solution: 0.30 *is greater than* 0.03, because the tenth place of 0.30 is 3, but the tenth place of 0.03 is zero. Then: 0.03 < 0.30

Example 2. Compare 0.0217 and 0.217.

Solution: 0.217 *is greater than* 0.0217, because the tenth place of 0.217 is 2, but the tenth place of 0.0217 is zero. Then: 0.0217 < 0.217

bit.ly/2WHt2Za

Find more at

Rounding Decimals

- We can round decimals to a certain accuracy or number of decimal places. This is used to make calculations easier to do and results easier to understand when exact values are not too important.

- First, you'll need to remember your place values: For example: 12.4869

  1: tens   2: ones   4: tenths

  8: hundredths   6: thousandths   9: tens thousandths

- To round a decimal, first find the place value you'll round to.

- Find the digit to the right of the place value you're rounding to. If it is 5 or bigger, add 1 to the place value you're rounding to and remove all digits on its right side. If the digit to the right of the place value is less than 5, keep the place value and remove all digits on the right.

Examples:

Example 1. Round 4.3679 to the thousandth place value.

Solution: First, look at the next place value to the right, (tens thousandths). It's 9 and it is greater than 5. Thus add 1 to the digit in the thousandth place. The thousandth place is 7. $\rightarrow 7 + 1 = 8$, then,
The answer is 4.368

Example 2. Round 1.5237 to the nearest hundredth.

Solution: First, look at the digit to the right of hundredth (thousandths place value). It's 3 and it is less than 5, thus remove all the digits to the right of hundredth place. Then, the answer is 1.52

bit.ly/3mKEluf
Find more at

Adding and Subtracting Decimals

- Line up the decimal numbers.

- Add zeros to have the same number of digits for both numbers if necessary.

- Remember your place values: For example: 73.5196

  7: tens   3: ones   5: tenths

  1: hundredths   9: thousandths   6: tens thousandths

- Add or subtract using column addition or subtraction.

Examples:

Example 1. Add. $1.7 + 4.12$

Solution: First, line up the numbers: $\begin{array}{r} 1.7 \\ + 4.12 \\ \hline \end{array}$ → Add a zero to have the same number of digits for both numbers. $\begin{array}{r} 1.70 \\ + 4.12 \\ \hline \end{array}$ → Start with the hundredths place: $0 + 2 = 2$, $\begin{array}{r} 1.70 \\ + 4.12 \\ \hline 2 \end{array}$ → Continue with tenths place: $7 + 1 = 8$, $\begin{array}{r} 1.70 \\ + 4.12 \\ \hline .82 \end{array}$ → Add the ones place: $4 + 1 = 5$, $\begin{array}{r} 1.70 \\ + 4.12 \\ \hline 5.82 \end{array}$

Example 2. Find the difference. $5.58 - 4.23$

Solution: First, line up the numbers: $\begin{array}{r} 5.58 \\ - 4.23 \\ \hline \end{array}$ → Start with the hundredths place: $8 - 3 = 5$, $\begin{array}{r} 5.58 \\ - 4.23 \\ \hline 5 \end{array}$ → Continue with tenths place. $5 - 2 = 3$, $\begin{array}{r} 5.58 \\ - 4.23 \\ \hline .35 \end{array}$ → Subtract the ones place. $5 - 4 = 1$, $\begin{array}{r} 5.58 \\ - 4.23 \\ \hline 1.35 \end{array}$

Multiplying and Dividing Decimals

For multiplying decimals:

- Ignore the decimal point and set up and multiply the numbers as you do with whole numbers.

- Count the total number of decimal places in both of the factors.

- Place the decimal point in the product.

For dividing decimals:

- If the divisor is not a whole number, move the decimal point to the right to make it a whole number. Do the same for the dividend.

- Divide similar to whole numbers.

Examples:

Example 1. Find the product. $0.65 \times 0.24 =$

Solution: Set up and multiply the numbers as you do with whole numbers. Line up the numbers: $\begin{array}{r} 65 \\ \times\,24 \end{array}$ → Start with the ones place then continue with other digits $\rightarrow \begin{array}{r} 65 \\ \times 24 \\ \hline 1,560 \end{array}$. Count the total number of decimal places in both of the factors. There are four decimals digits. (two for each factor 0.65 and 0.24) Then: $0.65 \times 0.24 = 0.1560$

Example 2. Find the quotient. $1.20 \div 0.4 =$

Solution: The divisor is not a whole number. Multiply it by 10 to get 4: → $0.4 \times 10 = 4$

Do the same for the dividend to get 12. → $1.20 \times 10 = 12$

Now, divide $12 \div 4 = 3$. The answer is 3.

Chapter 2: Practices

✎ Compare. Use >, =, and <

1) 0.5 ☐ 0.6

2) 0.9 ☐ 0.8

3) 0.1 ☐ 0.2

4) 0.02 ☐ 0.06

5) 0.05 ☐ 0.08

6) 0.12 ☐ 0.09

7) 3.2 ☐ 2.5

8) 4.8 ☐ 8.4

9) 0.005 ☐ 0.05

10) 2.02 ☐ 20.020

11) 55.100 ☐ 55.10

12) 0.44 ☐ 0.440

13) 6.01 ☐ 6.0100

14) 0.77 ☐ 77.0

✎ Round each decimal to the nearest whole number.

15) 5.8

16) 6.4

17) 12.3

18) 9.2

19) 7.6

20) 22.4

21) 6.8

22) 15.9

23) 13.41

24) 16.78

25) 67.58

26) 42.67

27) 55.89

28) 14.32

29) 78.88

30) 98.29

✎ Find the sum or difference.

31) $12.1 + 36.2 =$

32) $56.3 - 22.2 =$

33) $45.1 + 12.8 =$

34) $27.9 - 16.4 =$

35) $98.8 - 56.6 =$

36) $28.45 + 13.22 =$

37) $16.78 + 45.11 =$

38) $86.16 - 72.12 =$

39) $96.23 - 28.32 =$

40) $57.33 + 67.46 =$

41) $46.26 - 39.49 =$

42) $44.95 + 76.53 =$

43) $79.37 - 52.89 =$

44) $19.99 + 28.7 =$

45) $83.48 - 49.3 =$

46) $19.6 + 42.98 =$

✎ Find the product or quotient.

47) $3.3 \times 0.2 =$

48) $2.4 \div 0.3 =$

49) $8.1 \times 1.4 =$

50) $4.8 \div 0.2 =$

51) $4.1 \times 0.3 =$

52) $8.6 \div 0.2 =$

53) $9.9 \times 0.8 =$

54) $1.84 \div 0.2 =$

55) $2.1 \times 8.4 =$

56) $1.6 \times 4.5 =$

57) $9.2 \times 3.1 =$

58) $36.6 \div 1.6 =$

59) $1.91 \times 5.2 =$

60) $3.65 \times 1.4 =$

61) $24.82 \div 0.4 =$

62) $12.4 \times 4.20 =$

Effortless
Math
Education

Chapter 2: Answers

1)	<	22)	16	43)	26.48
2)	>	23)	13	44)	48.69
3)	<	24)	17	45)	34.18
4)	<	25)	68	46)	62.58
5)	<	26)	43	47)	0.66
6)	>	27)	56	48)	8
7)	>	28)	14	49)	11.34
8)	<	29)	79	50)	24
9)	<	30)	98	51)	1.23
10)	<	31)	48.3	52)	43
11)	=	32)	34.1	53)	7.92
12)	=	33)	57.9	54)	9.2
13)	=	34)	11.5	55)	17.64
14)	<	35)	42.2	56)	7.2
15)	6	36)	41.67	57)	28.52
16)	6	37)	61.89	58)	22.875
17)	12	38)	14.04	59)	9.932
18)	9	39)	67.91	60)	5.11
19)	8	40)	124.79	61)	62.05
20)	22	41)	6.77	62)	52.08
21)	7	42)	121.48		

Effortless
Math
Education

CHAPTER

3 Integers and Order of Operations

Math topics that you'll learn in this chapter:

☑ Adding and Subtracting Integers

☑ Multiplying and Dividing Integers

☑ Order of Operations

☑ Integers and Absolute Value

Adding and Subtracting Integers

- Integers include zero, counting numbers, and the negative of the counting numbers. $\{\ldots, -3, -2, -1, 0, 1, 2, 3, \ldots\}$

- Add a positive integer by moving to the right on the number line. (you will get a bigger number)

- Add a negative integer by moving to the left on the number line. (you will get a smaller number)

- Subtract an integer by adding its opposite.

Examples:

Example 1. Solve. $(-2) - (-8) =$

Solution: Keep the first number and convert the sign of the second number to its opposite. (change subtraction into addition. Then: $(-2) + 8 = 6$

Example 2. Solve. $4 + (5 - 10) =$

Solution: First, subtract the numbers in brackets, $5 - 10 = -5$.
Then: $4 + (-5) = \;\rightarrow$ change addition into subtraction: $4 - 5 = -1$

Example 3. Solve. $(9 - 14) + 15 =$

Solution: First, subtract the numbers in brackets, $9 - 14 = -5$
Then: $-5 + 15 = \;\rightarrow -5 + 15 = 10$

Example 4. Solve. $12 + (-3 - 10) =$

Solution: First, subtract the numbers in brackets, $-3 - 10 = -13$
Then: $12 + (-13) = \;\rightarrow$ change addition into subtraction: $12 - 13 = -1$

Unterscheidung

Multiplying and Dividing Integers

Use the following rules for multiplying and dividing integers:

- (negative) × (negative) = positive

- (negative) ÷ (negative) = positive

- (negative) × (positive) = negative

- (negative) ÷ (positive) = negative

- (positive) × (positive) = positive

- (positive) ÷ (negative) = negative

Examples:

Example 1. Solve. $3 \times (-4) =$

Solution: Use this rule: (positive) × (negative) = negative.
Then: $(3) \times (-4) = -12$

Example 2. Solve. $(-3) + (-24 \div 3) =$

Solution: First, divide -24 by 3, the numbers in brackets, use this rule:
(negative) ÷ (positive) = negative. Then: $-24 \div 3 = -8$
$(-3) + (-24 \div 3) = (-3) + (-8) = -3 - 8 = -11$

Example 3. Solve. $(12 - 15) \times (-2) =$

Solution: First, subtract the numbers in brackets,
$12 - 15 = -3 \rightarrow (-3) \times (-2) =$
Now use this rule: (negative) × (negative) = positive $\rightarrow (-3) \times (-2) = 6$

Example 4. Solve. $(12 - 8) \div (-4) =$

Solution: First, subtract the numbers in brackets,
$12 - 8 = 4 \rightarrow (4) \div (-4) =$
Now use this rule: (positive) ÷ (negative) = negative $\rightarrow (4) \div (-4) =$
-1

Order of Operations

- In Mathematics, "operations" are addition, subtraction, multiplication, division, exponentiation (written as b^n), and grouping.

- When there is more than one math operation in an expression, use PEMDAS: (to memorize this rule, remember the phrase "Please Excuse My Dear Aunt Sally".)

- ❖ Parentheses
- ❖ Exponents
- ❖ Multiplication and Division (from left to right)
- ❖ Addition and Subtraction (from left to right)

Examples:

Example 1. Calculate. $(2 + 6) \div (2^2 \div 4) =$

Solution: First, simplify inside parentheses:
$(8) \div (4 \div 4) = (8) \div (1)$, Then: $(8) \div (1) = 8$

Example 2. Solve. $(6 \times 5) - (14 - 5) =$

Solution: First, calculate within parentheses: $(6 \times 5) - (14 - 5) = (30) - (9)$, Then: $(30) - (9) = 21$

Example 3. Calculate. $-4[(3 \times 6) \div (3^2 \times 2)] =$

Solution: First, calculate within parentheses:
$-4[(18) \div (9 \times 2)] = -4[(18) \div (18)] = -4[1]$
multiply -4 and 1. Then: $-4[1] = -4$

Example 4. Solve. $(28 \div 7) + (-19 + 3) =$

Solution: First, calculate within parentheses:
$(28 \div 7) + (-19 + 3) = (4) + (-16)$ Then: $(4) - (16) = -12$

bit.ly/37LBw7X

Find more at

Integers and Absolute Value

- The absolute value of a number is its distance from zero, in either direction, on the number line. For example, the distance of 9 and -9 from zero on number line is 9.

- The absolute value of an integer is the numerical value without its sign. (negative or positive)

- The vertical bar is used for absolute value as in $|x|$.

- The absolute value of a number is never negative; because it only shows, "how far the number is from zero".

Examples:

Example 1. Calculate. $|14 - 2| \times 5 =$

Solution: First, solve $|14 - 2|$, $\rightarrow |14 - 2| = |12|$, the absolute value of 12 is 12, $|12| = 12$ Then: $12 \times 5 = 60$

Example 2. Solve. $\frac{|-24|}{4} \times |5 - 7| =$

Solution: First, find $|-24|$, $\rightarrow$ the absolute value of -24 is 24,
Then: $|-24| = 24$, $\frac{24}{4} \times |5 - 7| =$
Now, calculate $|5 - 7|$, $\rightarrow |5 - 7| = |-2|$, the absolute value of -2 is 2. $|-2| = 2$
then: $\frac{24}{4} \times 2 = 6 \times 2 = 12$

Example 3. Solve. $|8 - 2| \times \frac{|-4 \times 7|}{2} =$

Solution: First, calculate $|8 - 2|$, $\rightarrow |8 - 2| = |6|$, the absolute value of 6 is 6, $|6| = 6$. Then: $6 \times \frac{|-4 \times 7|}{2}$
Now calculate $|-4 \times 7|$, $\rightarrow |-4 \times 7| = |-28|$, the absolute value of -28 is 28, $|-28| = 28$ Then: $6 \times \frac{28}{2} = 6 \times 14 = 84$

bit.ly/3aD521u
Find more at

Chapter 3: Practices

✎ Find each sum or difference.

1) $-9 + 16 =$

2) $-18 - 6 =$

3) $-24 + 10 =$

4) $30 + (-5) =$

5) $15 + (-3) =$

6) $(-13) + (-4) =$

7) $25 + (3 - 10) =$

8) $12 - (-6 + 9) =$

9) $5 - (-2 + 7) =$

10) $(-11) + (-5 + 6) =$

11) $(-3) + (9 - 16) =$

12) $(-8) - (13 + 4) =$

13) $(-7 + 9) - 39 =$

14) $(-30 + 6) - 14 =$

15) $(-5 + 9) + (-3 + 7) =$

16) $(8 - 19) - (-4 + 12) =$

17) $(-9 + 2) - (6 - 7) =$

18) $(-12 - 5) - (-4 - 14) =$

✎ Solve.

19) $3 \times (-6) =$

20) $(-32) \div 4 =$

21) $(-5) \times 4 =$

22) $(25) \div (-5) =$

23) $(-72) \div 8 =$

24) $(-2) \times (-6) \times 5 =$

25) $(-2) \times 3 \times (-7) =$

26) $(-1) \times (-3) \times (-5) =$

27) $(-2) \times (-3) \times (-6) =$

28) $(-12 + 3) \times (-5) =$

29) $(-3 + 4) \times (-11) =$

30) $(-9) \times (6 - 5) =$

31) $(-3 - 7) \times (-6) =$

32) $(-7 + 3) \times (-9 + 6) =$

33) $(-15) \div (-17 + 12) =$

34) $(-3 - 2) \times (-9 + 7) =$

35) $(-15 + 31) \div (-2) =$

36) $(-64) \div (-16 + 8) =$

✎ Evaluate each expression.

37) $3 + (2 \times 5) =$

38) $(5 \times 4) - 7 =$

39) $(-9 \times 2) + 6 =$

40) $(7 \times 3) - (-5) =$

41) $(-8) + (2 \times 7) =$

42) $(9 - 6) + (3 \times 4) =$

43) $(-19 + 5) + (6 \times 2) =$

44) $(32 \div 4) + (1 - 13) =$

45) $(-36 \div 6) - (12 + 3) =$

46) $(-16 + 5) - (54 \div 9) =$

47) $(-20 + 4) - (35 \div 5) =$

48) $(42 \div 7) + (2 \times 3) =$

49) $(28 \div 4) + (2 \times 6) =$

50) $2[(3 \times 3) - (4 \times 5)] =$

51) $3[(2 \times 8) + (4 \times 3)] =$

52) $2[(9 \times 3) - (6 \times 4)] =$

53) $4[(4 \times 8) \div (4 \times 4)] =$

54) $-5[(10 \times 8) \div (5 \times 8)] =$

✎ Find the answers.

55) $|-5| + |7 - 10| =$

56) $|-4 + 6| + |-2| =$

57) $|-9| + |1 - 9| =$

58) $|-7| - |8 - 12| =$

59) $|9 - 11| + |8 - 15| =$

60) $|-7 + 10| - |-8 + 3| =$

61) $|-12 + 6| - |3 - 9| =$

62) $5 + |2 - 6| + |3 - 4| =$

63) $-4 + |2 - 6| + |1 - 9| =$

64) $|-6| \times |-7| + |2 - 8| =$

65) $|-12| \times |-3| + |4 - 28| =$

66) $|4 \times (-2)| \times |-9| =$

67) $|-3 \times 2| \times |-5| =$

68) $|3 - 12| - |-3 \times 7| =$

69) $|-9| + |-7 \times 5| =$

70) $|-11| + |-6 \times 4| =$

71) $|-4 \times 2 + 6| \times |-2 \times 8| =$

72) $|-1 \times 5 + 2| \times |-4| =$

Effortless
Math
Education

Chapter 3: Answers

1)	7	25)	42	49)	19
2)	−24	26)	−15	50)	−22
3)	−14	27)	−36	51)	84
4)	25	28)	45	52)	6
5)	12	29)	−11	53)	8
6)	−17	30)	−9	54)	−10
7)	18	31)	60	55)	8
8)	9	32)	12	56)	4
9)	0	33)	3	57)	17
10)	−10	34)	10	58)	3
11)	−10	35)	−8	59)	9
12)	−25	36)	8	60)	−2
13)	−37	37)	13	61)	0
14)	−38	38)	13	62)	10
15)	8	39)	−12	63)	8
16)	−19	40)	26	64)	48
17)	−6	41)	6	65)	60
18)	1	42)	15	66)	72
19)	−18	43)	−2	67)	30
20)	−8	44)	−4	68)	−12
21)	−20	45)	−21	69)	44
22)	−5	46)	−17	70)	35
23)	−9	47)	−23	71)	32
24)	60	48)	12	72)	12

4 Ratios and Proportions

Math topics that you'll learn in this chapter:

- ☑ Simplifying Ratios
- ☑ Proportional Ratios
- ☑ Similarity and Ratios

Simplifying Ratios

- Ratios are used to make comparisons between two numbers.

- Ratios can be written as a fraction, using the word "to", or with a colon.
  Example: $\frac{3}{4}$ or "3 to 4" or 3:4

- You can calculate equivalent ratios by multiplying or dividing both sides of the ratio by the same number.

Examples:

Example 1. Simplify. $8:2 =$

Solution: Both numbers 8 and 2 are divisible by 2 , $\Rightarrow 8 \div 2 = 4$,
$4 \div 2 = 2$, Then: $8:2 = 4:1$

Example 2. Simplify. $\frac{9}{33} =$

Solution: Both numbers 9 and 33 are divisible by 3, $\Rightarrow 33 \div 3 = 11$, $9 \div 3 = 3$,
Then: $\frac{9}{33} = \frac{3}{11}$

Example 3. There are 24 students in a class and 10 are girls. Write the ratio of girls to boys.

Solution: Subtract 10 from 24 to find the number of boys in the class.
$24 - 10 = 14$. There are 14 boys in the class. So, the ratio of girls to boys is $10:14$.
Now, simplify this ratio. Both 14 and 10 are divisible by 2.
Then: $14 \div 2 = 7$, and $10 \div 2 = 5$. In the simplest form, this ratio is $5:7$

Example 4. A recipe calls for butter and sugar in the ratio $3:4$. If you're using 9 cups of butter, how many cups of sugar should you use?

Solution: Since you use 9 cups of butter, or 3 times as much, you need to multiply the amount of sugar by 3. Then: $4 \times 3 = 12$. So, you need to use 12 cups of sugar. You can solve this using equivalent fractions: $\frac{3}{4} = \frac{9}{12}$

bit.ly/3nKwq0Z
Find more at

Proportional Ratios

- Two ratios are proportional if they represent the same relationship.

- A proportion means that two ratios are equal. It can be written in two ways: $\frac{a}{b} = \frac{c}{d}$ $a : b = c : d$

- The proportion $\frac{a}{b} = \frac{c}{d}$ can be written as: $a \times d = c \times b$

Examples:

Example 1. Solve this proportion for x. $\frac{2}{5} = \frac{6}{x}$

Solution: Use cross multiplication: $\frac{2}{5} = \frac{6}{x} \Rightarrow 2 \times x = 6 \times 5 \Rightarrow 2x = 30$

Divide both sides by 2 to find x: $x = \frac{30}{2} \Rightarrow x = 15$

Example 2. If a box contains red and blue balls in ratio of $3 : 5$ red to blue, how many red balls are there if 45 blue balls are in the box?

Solution: Write a proportion and solve. $\frac{3}{5} = \frac{x}{45}$

Use cross multiplication: $3 \times 45 = 5 \times x \Rightarrow 135 = 5x$

Divide to find x: $x = \frac{135}{5} \Rightarrow x = 27$. There are 27 red balls in the box.

Example 3. Solve this proportion for x. $\frac{4}{9} = \frac{16}{x}$

Solution: Use cross multiplication: $\frac{4}{9} = \frac{16}{x} \Rightarrow 4 \times x = 9 \times 16 \Rightarrow 4x = 144$

Divide to find x: $x = \frac{144}{4} \Rightarrow x = 36$

Example 4. Solve this proportion for x. $\frac{5}{7} = \frac{20}{x}$

Solution: Use cross multiplication: $\frac{5}{7} = \frac{20}{x} \Rightarrow 5 \times x = 7 \times 20 \Rightarrow 5x = 140$

Divide to find x: $x = \frac{140}{5} \Rightarrow x = 28$

bit.ly/37GHQxp

Find more at

Similarity and Ratios

- Two figures are similar if they have the same shape.

- Two or more figures are similar if the corresponding angles are equal, and the corresponding sides are in proportion.

Examples:

Example 1. The following triangles are similar. What is the value of the unknown side?

Example 2.

Solution: Find the corresponding sides and write a proportion.

$\frac{8}{16} = \frac{6}{x}$. Now, use the cross product to solve for x:

$\frac{8}{16} = \frac{6}{x} \rightarrow 8 \times x = 16 \times 6 \rightarrow 8x = 96$. Divide both sides by 8. Then: $8x = 96 \rightarrow x = \frac{96}{8} \rightarrow x = 12$

The missing side is 12.

Example 3. Two rectangles are similar. The first is 5 feet wide and 15 feet long. The second is 10 feet wide. What is the length of the second rectangle?

Solution: Let's put x for the length of the second rectangle. Since two rectangles are similar, their corresponding sides are in proportion. Write a proportion and solve for the missing number.

$\frac{5}{10} = \frac{15}{x} \rightarrow 5x = 10 \times 15 \rightarrow 5x = 150 \rightarrow x = \frac{150}{5} = 30$

The length of the second rectangle is 30 feet.

bit.ly/2KKKmcV

Find more at

Chapter 4: Practices

✍ Reduce each ratio.

1) $2:18 = $ ___: ___

2) $5:35 = $ ___: ___

3) $8:72 = $ ___: ___

4) $24:36 = $ ___: ___

5) $25:40 = $ ___: ___

6) $40:72 = $ ___: ___

7) $28:63 = $ ___: ___

8) $18:81 = $ ___: ___

9) $13:52 = $ ___: ___

10) $56:72 = $ ___: ___

11) $42:63 = $ ___: ___

12) $32:96 = $ ___: ___

✍ Solve.

13) Bob has 16 red cards and 20 green cards. What is the ratio of Bob's red cards to his green cards? _____

14) In a party, 34 soft drinks are required for every 20 guests. If there are 260 guests, how many soft drinks are required? _____

15) Sara has 56 blue pens and 28 black pens. What is the ratio of Sara's black pens to her blue pens? _____

16) In Jack's class, 48 of the students are tall and 20 are short. In Michael's class 28 students are tall and 12 students are short. Which class has a higher ratio of tall to short students? _____

17) The price of 6 apples at the Quick Market is $1.52. The price of 5 of the same apples at Walmart is $1.32. Which place is the better buy? _____

18) The bakers at a Bakery can make 180 bagels in 6 hours. How many bagels can they bake in 16 hours? What is that rate per hour? _____

19) You can buy 6 cans of green beans at a supermarket for $3.48. How much does it cost to buy 38 cans of green beans? _____

Effortless
Math
Education

✎ Solve each proportion.

20) $\frac{3}{2} = \frac{9}{x} \Rightarrow x = $ ____

21) $\frac{7}{2} = \frac{x}{4} \Rightarrow x = $ ____

22) $\frac{1}{3} = \frac{2}{x} \Rightarrow x = $ ____

23) $\frac{1}{4} = \frac{5}{x} \Rightarrow x = $ ____

24) $\frac{9}{6} = \frac{x}{2} \Rightarrow x = $ ____

25) $\frac{3}{6} = \frac{5}{x} \Rightarrow x = $ ____

26) $\frac{7}{x} = \frac{2}{6} \Rightarrow x = $ ____

27) $\frac{2}{x} = \frac{4}{10} \Rightarrow x = $ ____

28) $\frac{3}{2} = \frac{x}{8} \Rightarrow x = $ ____

29) $\frac{x}{6} = \frac{5}{3} \Rightarrow x = $ ____

30) $\frac{3}{9} = \frac{5}{x} \Rightarrow x = $ ____

31) $\frac{4}{18} = \frac{2}{x} \Rightarrow x = $ ____

32) $\frac{6}{16} = \frac{3}{x} \Rightarrow x = $ ____

33) $\frac{2}{5} = \frac{x}{20} \Rightarrow x = $ ____

34) $\frac{28}{8} = \frac{x}{2} \Rightarrow x = $ ____

35) $\frac{3}{5} = \frac{x}{15} \Rightarrow x = $ ____

36) $\frac{2}{7} = \frac{x}{14} \Rightarrow x = $ ____

37) $\frac{x}{18} = \frac{3}{2} \Rightarrow x = $ ____

38) $\frac{x}{24} = \frac{2}{6} \Rightarrow x = $ ____

39) $\frac{5}{x} = \frac{4}{20} \Rightarrow x = $ ____

40) $\frac{10}{x} = \frac{20}{80} \Rightarrow x = $ ____

41) $\frac{90}{6} = \frac{x}{2} \Rightarrow x = $ ____

✎ Solve each problem.

42) Two rectangles are similar. The first is 8 *feet* wide and 32 *feet* long. The second is 12 *feet* wide. What is the length of the second rectangle?

_____

43) Two rectangles are similar. One is 4.6 *meters* by 7 *meters*. The longer side of the second rectangle is 28 *meters*. What is the other side of the second rectangle? _____

Chapter 4: Answers

1) $1:9$

2) $1:7$

3) $1:9$

4) $2:3$

5) $5:8$

6) $5:9$

7) $4:9$

8) $2:9$

9) $1:4$

10) $7:9$

11) $2:3$

12) $1:3$

13) $4:5$

14) 442

15) $1:2$

16) $Jack's\ class: \frac{48}{20} = \frac{12}{5}$ $Michael's\ class: \frac{28}{12} = \frac{7}{3}$ Jack's class has a higher ratio of tall to short student: $\frac{12}{5} > \frac{7}{3}$

17) Quick market

18) 480, 30 bagels per hour

19) $22.04

20) 6

21) 14

22) 6

23) 20

24) 3

25) 10

26) 21

27) 5

28) 12

29) 10

30) 15

31) 9

32) 8

33) 8

34) 7

35) 9

36) 4

37) 27

38) 8

39) 25

40) 40

41) 30

42) $48\ feet$

43) $18.4\ meters$

Effortless Math Education

CHAPTER

5 Percentage

Math topics that you'll learn in this chapter:

☑ Percent Problems

☑ Percent of Increase and Decrease

☑ Discount, Tax and Tip

☑ Simple Interest

Percent Problems

-   Percent is a ratio of a number and 100. It always has the same denominator, 100. The percent symbol is "%".

-   Percent means "per 100". So, 20% is 20/100.

-   In each percent problem, we are looking for the base, or part or the percent.

-   Use these equations to find each missing section in a percent problem:

    ❖   Base = Part ÷ Percent

    ❖   Part = Percent × Base

    ❖   Percent = Part ÷ Base

Examples:

Example 1. What is 20% of 40?

Solution: In this problem, we have percent (20%) and base (40) and we are looking for the "part". Use this formula: $part = percent \times base$.

Then: $part = 20\% \times 40 = \frac{20}{100} \times 40 = 0.20 \times 40 = 8$. The answer: 20% of 40 is 8.

Example 2. 25 is what percent of 500?

Solution: In this problem, we are looking for the percent. Use this equation: $Percent = Part \div Base \rightarrow Percent = 25 \div 500 = 0.05 = 5\%$.

Then: 25 is 5 percent of 500.

Percent of Increase and Decrease

- Percent of change (increase or decrease) is a mathematical concept that represents the degree of change over time.

- To find the percentage of increase or decrease:

    1. New Number – Original Number

    2. The result ÷ Original Number × 100

- Or use this formula: Percent of change $= \frac{new\ number - original\ number}{original\ number} \times 100$

- Note: If your answer is a negative number, then this is a percentage decrease. If it is positive, then this is a percentage increase.

Examples:

Example 1. The price of a shirt increases from \$30 to \$40. What is the percentage increase?

Solution: First, find the difference: $40 - 30 = 10$

Then: $10 \div 30 \times 100 = \frac{10}{30} \times 100 = 33.33$. The percentage increase is 33.33. It means that the price of the shirt increased by 33.33%.

Example 2. The price of a table increased from \$20 to \$50. What is the percent of increase?

Solution: Use percentage formula:

$Percent\ of\ change = \frac{new\ number - original\ number}{original\ number} \times 100 =$

$\frac{50-20}{20} \times 100 = \frac{30}{20} \times 100 = 1.5 \times 100 = 150$. The percentage increase is 150. It means that the price of the table increased by 150%.

bit.ly/3pgPQes
Find more at

Discount, Tax and Tip

- To find the discount: Multiply the regular price by the rate of discount

- To find the selling price: Original price – discount

- To find tax: Multiply the tax rate to the taxable amount (income, property value, etc.)

- To find the tip, multiply the rate to the selling price.

Examples:

Example 1. With an 20% discount, Ella saved $50 on a dress. What was the original price of the dress?

Solution: let x be the original price of the dress. Then: $20\% \; of \; x = 50$. Write an equation and solve for x: $0.20 \times x = 50 \rightarrow x = \frac{50}{0.20} = 250$. The original price of the dress was $250.

Example 2. Sophia purchased a new computer for a price of $820 at the Apple Store. What is the total amount her credit card is charged if the sales tax is 5%?

Solution: The taxable amount is $820, and the tax rate is 5%. Then: $Tax = 0.05 \times 820 = 41$
$Final \; price = Selling \; price + Tax \rightarrow final \; price = \$820 + \$41 = \$861$

Example 3. Nicole and her friends went out to eat at a restaurant. If their bill was $60.00 and they gave their server a 15% tip, how much did they pay altogether?

Solution: First, find the tip. To find the tip, multiply the rate to the bill amount. $Tip = 60 \times 0.15 = 9$. The final price is: $\$60 + \$9 = \$69$

bit.ly/2Je5lo0

Find more at

Simple Interest

- Simple Interest: The charge for borrowing money or the return for lending it.

- Simple interest is calculated on the initial amount (principal).

- To solve a simple interest problem, use this formula:

Interest = principal × rate × time $(I = p \times r \times t = prt)$

Examples:

Example 1. Find simple interest for $200 investment at 5% for 3 years.

Solution: Use Interest formula:
$I = prt$ ($P = \$200$, r = 5% $= \frac{5}{100} = 0.05$ and $t = 3$)
Then: $I = 200 \times 0.05 \times 3 = \$30$

Example 2. Find simple interest for $1,200 at 8% for 6 years.

Solution: Use Interest formula:
$I = prt$ ($P = \$1,200$, r = 8% $= \frac{8}{100} = 0.08$ and $t = 6$)
Then: $I = 1,200 \times 0.08 \times 6 = \$576$

Example 3. Andy received a student loan to pay for his educational expenses this year. What is the interest on the loan if he borrowed $4,500 at 6% for 5 years?

Solution: Use Interest formula: $I = prt$. $P = \$4,500$, r = 6% $= 0.06$ and $t = 5$
Then: $I = 4,500 \times 0.06 \times 5 = \$1,350$

Example 4. Bob is starting his own small business. He borrowed $20,000 from the bank at a 8% rate for 6 months. Find the interest Bob will pay on this loan.

Solution: Use Interest formula:
$I = prt$. $P = \$20,000$, r = 8% $= 0.08$ and $t = 0.5$ (6 months is half year). Then: $I = 20,000 \times 0.08 \times 0.5 = \$800$

Chapter 5: Practices

✍ Solve each problem.

1) What is 15% of 60? ____

2) What is 55% of 800? ____

3) What is 22% of 120? ____

4) What is 18% of 40? ____

5) 90 is what percent of 200? ____%

6) 30 is what percent of 150? ____%

7) 14 is what percent of 250? ____%

8) 60 is what percent of 300? ____%

9) 30 is 120 percent of what number? ____

10) 120 is 20 percent of what number? ____

11) 15 is 5 percent of what number? ____

12) 22 is 20% of what number? ____

✍ Solve each problem.

13) Bob got a raise, and his hourly wage increased from $15 to $21. What is the percent increase? _____ %

14) The price of a pair of shoes increases from $32 to $36. What is the percent increase? ___ %

15) At a Coffee Shop, the price of a cup of coffee increased from $1.35 to $1.62. What is the percent increase in the cost of the coffee? _____ %

16) A $45 shirt now selling for $36 is discounted by what percent? _____ %

17) Joe scored 30 out of 35 marks in Algebra, 20 out of 30 marks in science and 58 out of 70 marks in mathematics. In which subject his percentage of marks is best? _____

18) Emma purchased a computer for $420. The computer is regularly priced at $480. What was the percent discount Emma received on the computer? _____

19) A chemical solution contains 15% alcohol. If there is 54 ml of alcohol, what is the volume of the solution? _____

Effortless
Math
Education

Find the selling price of each item.

20) Original price of a computer: $600

Tax: 8%, Selling price: $_____

21) Original price of a laptop: $450

Tax: 10%, Selling price: $_____

22) Nicolas hired a moving company. The company charged $500 for its services, and Nicolas gives the movers a 14% tip. How much does Nicolas tip the movers? $_____

23) Mason has lunch at a restaurant and the cost of his meal is $40. Mason wants to leave a 20% tip. What is Mason's total bill, including tip? $_____

Determine the simple interest for the following loans.

24) $1,000 *at* 5% *for* 4 *years.* $__

25) $400 *at* 3% *for* 5 *years.* $__

26) $240 *at* 4% *for* 3 *years.* $__

27) $500 at 4.5% for 6 years. $__

Solve.

28) A new car, valued at $20,000, depreciates at 8% per year. What is the value of the car one year after purchase? $_____

29) Sara puts $7,000 into an investment yielding 3% annual simple interest; she left the money in for five years. How much interest does Sara get at the end of those five years? $_____

Effortless
Math
Education

Chapter 5: Answers

1)	9	16)	20%
2)	440	17)	Algebra
3)	26.4	18)	12.5%
4)	7.2	19)	360 ml
5)	45%	20)	$648.00
6)	20%	21)	$495.00
7)	5.6%	22)	$70.00
8)	20%	23)	$48.00
9)	25	24)	$200.00
10)	600	25)	$60.00
11)	300	26)	$28.80
12)	110	27)	$135.00
13)	40%	28)	$18.400
14)	12.5%	29)	$1,050
15)	20%		

CHAPTER

6 Exponents and Variables

Math topics that you'll learn in this chapter:

- ☑ Multiplication Property of Exponents
- ☑ Division Property of Exponents
- ☑ Powers of Products and Quotients
- ☑ Zero and Negative Exponents
- ☑ Negative Exponents and Negative Bases
- ☑ Scientific Notation
- ☑ Radicals

Multiplication Property of Exponents

- Exponents are shorthand for repeated multiplication of the same number by itself. For example, instead of 2×2, we can write 2^2. For $3 \times 3 \times 3 \times 3$, we can write 3^4

- In algebra, a variable is a letter used to stand for a number. The most common letters are: $x, y, z, a, b, c, m,$ and n.

- Exponent's rules: $x^a \times x^b = x^{a+b}$, $\dfrac{x^a}{x^b} = x^{a-b}$

$$(x^a)^b = x^{a \times b} \qquad\qquad (xy)^a = x^a \times y^a \qquad\qquad \left(\dfrac{a}{b}\right)^c = \dfrac{a^c}{b^c}$$

Examples:

Example 1. Multiply. $2x^2 \times 3x^4$

Solution: Use Exponent's rules: $x^a \times x^b = x^{a+b} \rightarrow x^2 \times x^4 = x^{2+4} = x^6$
Then: $2x^2 \times 3x^4 = 6x^6$

Example 2. Simplify. $(x^4 y^2)^2$

Solution: Use Exponent's rules: $(x^a)^b = x^{a \times b}$.
Then: $(x^4 y^2)^2 = x^{4 \times 2} y^{2 \times 2} = x^8 y^4$

Example 3. Multiply. $5x^8 \times 6x^5$

Solution: Use Exponent's rules: $x^a \times x^b = x^{a+b} \rightarrow x^8 \times x^5 = x^{8+5} = x^{13}$
Then: $5x^8 \times 6x^5 = 30x^{13}$

Example 4. Simplify. $(x^4 y^7)^3$

Solution: Use Exponent's rules: $(x^a)^b = x^{a \times b}$.
Then: $(x^4 y^7)^3 = x^{4 \times 3} y^{7 \times 3} = x^{12} y^{21}$

Division Property of Exponents

- Exponents are shorthand for repeated multiplication of the same number by itself. For example, instead of 3×3, we can write 3^2. For $2 \times 2 \times 2$, we can write 2^3

- For division of exponents use following formulas:

$$\frac{x^a}{x^b} = x^{a-b}, \; x \neq 0, \; \frac{x^a}{x^b} = \frac{1}{x^{b-a}}, \; x \neq 0, \qquad \frac{1}{x^b} = x^{-b}$$

Examples:

Example 1. Simplify. $\frac{16x^3y}{2xy^2} =$

Solution: First, cancel the common factor: $2 \rightarrow \frac{16x^3y}{2xy^2} = \frac{8x^3y}{xy^2}$

Use Exponent's rules: $\frac{x^a}{x^b} = x^{a-b} \rightarrow \frac{x^3}{x} = x^{3-1} = x^2$ and $\frac{y}{y^2} = \frac{1}{y^{2-1}} = \frac{1}{y}$

Then: $\frac{16x^3y}{2xy^2} = \frac{8x^2}{y}$

Example 2. Simplify. $\frac{24x^8}{3x^6} =$

Solution: Use Exponent's rules: $\frac{x^a}{x^b} = x^{b-a} \rightarrow \frac{x^8}{x^6} = x^{8-6} = x^2$

Then: $\frac{24x^8}{3x^6} = 8x^2$

Example 3. Simplify. $\frac{7x^4y^2}{28x^3y} =$

Solution: First, cancel the common factor: $7 \rightarrow \frac{x^4y^2}{4x^3y}$

Use Exponent's rules: $\frac{x^a}{x^b} = x^{a-b} \rightarrow \frac{x^4}{x^3} = x^{4-3} = x$ and $\frac{y^2}{y} = y$

Then: $\frac{7x^4y^2}{28x^3y} = \frac{xy}{4}$

Find more at bit.ly/37JAclZ

Powers of Products and Quotients

- Exponents are shorthand for repeated multiplication of the same number by itself. For example, instead of $2 \times 2 \times 2$, we can write 2^3. For $3 \times 3 \times 3 \times 3$, we can write 3^4

- For any nonzero numbers a and b and any integer x, $(ab)^x = a^x \times \mathrm{b}^x$ and $\left(\frac{a}{b}\right)^c = \frac{a^c}{b^c}$

Examples:

Example 1. Simplify. $(3x^3y^2)^2$

Solution: Use Exponent's rules: $(x^a)^b = x^{a \times b}$
$(3x^3y^2)^2 = (3)^2(x^3)^2(y^2)^2 = 9x^{3 \times 2}y^{2 \times 2} = 9x^6y^4$

Example 2. Simplify. $\left(\frac{2x^3}{3x^2}\right)^2$

Solution: First, cancel the common factor: $x \rightarrow \left(\frac{2x^3}{3x^2}\right) = \left(\frac{2x}{3}\right)^2$
Use Exponent's rules: $\left(\frac{a}{b}\right)^c = \frac{a^c}{b^c}$, Then: $\left(\frac{2x}{3}\right)^2 = \frac{(2x)^2}{(3)^2} = \frac{4x^2}{9}$

Example 3. Simplify. $\left(-4x^3y^5\right)^2$

Solution: Use Exponent's rules: $(x^a)^b = x^{a \times b}$
$$\left(-4x^3y^5\right)^2 = (-4)^2(x^3)^2\left(y^5\right)^2 = 16x^{3 \times 2}y^{5 \times 2} = 16x^6y^{10}$$

Example 4. Simplify. $\left(\frac{5x}{4x^2}\right)^2$

Solution: First, cancel the common factor: $x \rightarrow \left(\frac{5x}{4x^2}\right)^2 = \left(\frac{5}{4x}\right)^2$
Use Exponent's rules: $\left(\frac{a}{b}\right)^c = \frac{a^c}{b^c}$, Then: $\left(\frac{5}{4x}\right)^2 = \frac{5^2}{(4x)^2} = \frac{25}{16x^2}$

Zero and Negative Exponents

- Zero-Exponent Rule: $a^0 = 1$, this means that anything raised to the zero power is 1. For example: $(5xy)^0 = 1$

- A negative exponent simply means that the base is on the wrong side of the fraction line, so you need to flip the base to the other side. For instance, "x^{-2}" (pronounced as "ecks to the minus two") just means "x^2" but underneath, as in $\frac{1}{x^2}$.

Examples:

Example 1. Evaluate. $\left(\frac{4}{5}\right)^{-2} =$

Solution: Use negative exponent's rule: $\left(\frac{x^a}{x^b}\right)^{-2} = \left(\frac{x^b}{x^a}\right)^2 \rightarrow \left(\frac{4}{5}\right)^{-2} = \left(\frac{5}{4}\right)^2 =$
Then: $\left(\frac{5}{4}\right)^2 = \frac{5^2}{4^2} = \frac{25}{16}$

Example 2. Evaluate. $\left(\frac{3}{2}\right)^{-3} =$

Solution: Use negative exponent's rule: $\left(\frac{x^a}{x^b}\right)^{-3} = \left(\frac{x^b}{x^a}\right)^3 \rightarrow \left(\frac{3}{2}\right)^{-3} = \left(\frac{2}{3}\right)^3 =$
Then: $\left(\frac{2}{3}\right)^3 = \frac{2^3}{3^3} = \frac{8}{27}$

Example 3. Evaluate. $\left(\frac{a}{b}\right)^0 =$

Solution: Use zero-exponent Rule: $a^0 = 1$
Then: $\left(\frac{a}{b}\right)^0 = 1$

Example 4. Evaluate. $\left(\frac{4}{7}\right)^{-1} =$

Solution: Use negative exponent's rule: $\left(\frac{x^a}{x^b}\right)^{-1} = \left(\frac{x^b}{x^a}\right)^1 \rightarrow \left(\frac{4}{7}\right)^{-1} = \left(\frac{7}{4}\right)^1 = \frac{7}{4}$

bit.ly/3rnkh4v
Find more at

Negative Exponents and Negative Bases

- A negative exponent is the reciprocal of that number with a positive exponent. $(3)^{-2} = \frac{1}{3^2}$

- To simplify a negative exponent, make the power positive!

- The parenthesis is important! -5^{-2} is not the same as $(-5)^{-2}$

$$-5^{-2} = -\frac{1}{5^2} \text{ and } (-5)^{-2} = +\frac{1}{5^2}$$

Examples:

Example 1. Simplify. $\left(\frac{2a}{3c}\right)^{-2} =$

Solution: Use negative exponent's rule: $\left(\frac{x^a}{x^b}\right)^{-2} = \left(\frac{x^b}{x^a}\right)^2 \rightarrow \left(\frac{2a}{3c}\right)^{-2} = \left(\frac{3c}{2a}\right)^2$

Now use exponent's rule: $\left(\frac{a}{b}\right)^c = \frac{a^c}{b^c} \rightarrow = \left(\frac{3c}{2a}\right)^2 = \frac{3^2 c^2}{2^2 a^2}$

Then: $\frac{3^2 c^2}{2^2 a^2} = \frac{9c^2}{4a^2}$

Example 2. Simplify. $\left(\frac{x}{4y}\right)^{-3} =$

Solution: Use negative exponent's rule: $\left(\frac{x^a}{x^b}\right)^{-3} = \left(\frac{x^b}{x^a}\right)^3 \rightarrow \left(\frac{x}{4y}\right)^{-3} = \left(\frac{4y}{x}\right)^3$

Now use exponent's rule: $\left(\frac{a}{b}\right)^c = \frac{a^c}{b^c} \rightarrow \left(\frac{4y}{x}\right)^3 = \frac{4^3 y^3}{x^3} = \frac{64y^3}{x^3}$

Example 3. Simplify. $\left(\frac{5a}{2c}\right)^{-2} =$

Solution: Use negative exponent's rule: $\left(\frac{x^a}{x^b}\right)^{-2} = \left(\frac{x^b}{x^a}\right)^2 \rightarrow \left(\frac{5a}{2c}\right)^{-2} = \left(\frac{2c}{5a}\right)^2$

Now use exponent's rule: $\left(\frac{a}{b}\right)^c = \frac{a^c}{b^c} \rightarrow = \left(\frac{2c}{5a}\right)^2 = \frac{2^2 c^2}{5^2 a^2}$

Then: $\frac{2^2 c^2}{5^2 a^2} = \frac{4c^2}{25a^2}$

bit.ly/3nPROSM
Find more at

EffortlessMath.com

Scientific Notation

- Scientific notation is used to write very big or very small numbers in decimal form.

- In scientific notation, all numbers are written in the form of: $m \times 10^n$, where m is greater than 1 and less than 10.

- To convert a number from scientific notation to standard form, move the decimal point to the left (if the exponent of ten is a negative number), or to the right (if the exponent is positive).

Examples:

Example 1. Write 0.00024 in scientific notation.

Solution: First, move the decimal point to the right so you have a number between 1 and 10. That number is 2.4. Now, determine how many places the decimal moved in step 1 by the power of 10. We moved the decimal point 4 digits to the right. Then: $10^{-4} \rightarrow$ When the decimal moved to the right, the exponent is negative. Then: $0.00024 = 2.4 \times 10^{-4}$

Example 2. Write 3.8×10^{-5} in standard notation.

Solution: $10^{-5} \rightarrow$ When the decimal moved to the right, the exponent is negative. Then: $3.8 \times 10^{-5} = 0.000038$

Example 3. Write 0.00031 in scientific notation.

Solution: First, move the decimal point to the right so you have a number between 1 and 10. Then: $m = 3.1$, Now, determine how many places the decimal moved in step 1 by the power of 10.
$10^{-4} \rightarrow$ Then: $0.00031 = 3.1 \times 10^{-4}$

Example 4. Write 6.2×10^5 in standard notation.

Solution: $10^5 \rightarrow$ The exponent is positive 5. Then, move the decimal point to the right five digits. (remember $6.2 = 6.20000$),
Then: $6.2 \times 10^5 = 620000$

bit.ly/3nOwJYP

Find more at

Radicals

- If n is a positive integer and x is a real number, then: $\sqrt[n]{x} = x^{\frac{1}{n}}$,

$$\sqrt[n]{xy} = x^{\frac{1}{n}} \times y^{\frac{1}{n}}, \ \sqrt[n]{\frac{x}{y}} = \frac{x^{\frac{1}{n}}}{y^{\frac{1}{n}}}, \text{ and } \sqrt[n]{x} \times \sqrt[n]{y} = \sqrt[n]{xy}$$

- A square root of x is a number r whose square is: $r^2 = x$ (r is a square root of x)

- To add and subtract radicals, we need to have the same values under the radical. For example: $\sqrt{3} + \sqrt{3} = 2\sqrt{3}$, $3\sqrt{5} - \sqrt{5} = 2\sqrt{5}$

Examples:

Example 1. Find the square root of $\sqrt{121}$.

Solution: First, factor the number: $121 = 11^2$, Then: $\sqrt{121} = \sqrt{11^2}$, Now use radical rule: $\sqrt[n]{a^n} = a$. Then: $\sqrt{121} = \sqrt{11^2} = 11$

Example 2. Evaluate. $\sqrt{4} \times \sqrt{16} =$

Solution: Find the values of $\sqrt{4}$ and $\sqrt{16}$. Then: $\sqrt{4} \times \sqrt{16} = 2 \times 4 = 8$

Example 3. Solve. $5\sqrt{2} + 9\sqrt{2}$.

Solution: Since we have the same values under the radical, we can add these two radicals: $5\sqrt{2} + 9\sqrt{2} = 14\sqrt{2}$

Example 4. Evaluate. $\sqrt{2} \times \sqrt{50} =$

Solution: Use this radical rule: $\sqrt[n]{x} \times \sqrt[n]{y} = \sqrt[n]{xy} \rightarrow \sqrt{2} \times \sqrt{50} = \sqrt{100}$
The square root of 100 is 10. Then: $\sqrt{2} \times \sqrt{50} = \sqrt{100} = 10$

Chapter 6: Practices

✎ Find the products.

1) $x^2 \times 4xy^2 =$

2) $3x^2y \times 5x^3y^2 =$

3) $6x^4y^2 \times x^2y^3 =$

4) $7xy^3 \times 2x^2y =$

5) $-5x^5y^5 \times x^3y^2 =$

6) $-8x^3y^2 \times 3x^3y^2 =$

7) $-6x^2y^6 \times 5x^4y^2 =$

8) $-3x^3y^3 \times 2x^3y^2 =$

9) $-6x^5y^3 \times 4x^4y^3 =$

10) $-2x^4y^3 \times 5x^6y^2 =$

11) $-7y^6 \times 3x^6y^3 =$

12) $-9x^4 \times 2x^4y^2 =$

✎ Simplify.

13) $\frac{5^3 \times 5^4}{5^9 \times 5} =$

14) $\frac{3^3 \times 3^2}{7^2 \times 7} =$

15) $\frac{15x^5}{5x^3} =$

16) $\frac{16x^3}{4x^5} =$

17) $\frac{72y^2}{8x^3y^6} =$

18) $\frac{10x^3y^4}{50x^2y^3} =$

19) $\frac{13y^2}{52x^4y^4} =$

20) $\frac{50xy^3}{200x^3y^4} =$

21) $\frac{48x^2}{56x^2y^2} =$

22) $\frac{81y^6x}{54x^4y^3} =$

✎ Solve.

23) $(x^3y^3)^2 =$

24) $(3x^3y^4)^3 =$

25) $(4x \times 6xy^3)^2 =$

26) $(5x \times 2y^3)^3 =$

27) $\left(\frac{9x}{x^3}\right)^2 =$

28) $(\frac{3y}{18y^2})^2 =$

29) $\left(\frac{3x^2y^3}{24x^4y^2}\right)^3 =$

30) $\left(\frac{26x^5y^3}{52x^3y^5}\right)^2 =$

31) $\left(\frac{18x^7y^4}{72x^5y^2}\right)^2 =$

32) $\left(\frac{12x^6y^4}{48x^5y^3}\right)^2 =$

Effortless

Math

Education

✎ **Evaluate each expression. (Zero and Negative Exponents)**

33) $\left(\frac{1}{4}\right)^{-2} =$

34) $\left(\frac{1}{3}\right)^{-2} =$

35) $\left(\frac{1}{7}\right)^{-3} =$

36) $\left(\frac{2}{5}\right)^{-3} =$

37) $\left(\frac{2}{3}\right)^{-3} =$

38) $\left(\frac{3}{5}\right)^{-4} =$

✎ **Write each expression with positive exponents.**

39) $x^{-7} =$

40) $3y^{-5} =$

41) $15y^{-3} =$

42) $-20x^{-4} =$

43) $12a^{-3}b^5 =$

44) $25a^3b^{-4}c^{-3} =$

45) $-4x^5y^{-3}z^{-6} =$

46) $\frac{18y}{x^3y^{-2}} =$

47) $\frac{20a^{-2}b}{-12c^{-4}} =$

✎ **Write each number in scientific notation.**

48) $0.00412 =$

49) $0.000053 =$

50) $66,000 =$

51) $72,000,000 =$

✎ **Evaluate.**

52) $\sqrt{8} \times \sqrt{8} =$ ....

53) $\sqrt{36} - \sqrt{9} =$ ....

54) $\sqrt{81} + \sqrt{16} =$ ....

55) $\sqrt{4} \times \sqrt{25} =$ ....

56) $\sqrt{2} \times \sqrt{32} =$ ....

57) $4\sqrt{3} + 5\sqrt{3} =$ ....

Effortless

Math

Education

Chapter 6: Answers

1) $4x^3y^2$

2) $15x^5y^3$

3) $6x^6y^5$

4) $14x^3y^4$

5) $-5x^8y^7$

6) $-24x^6y^4$

7) $-30x^6y^8$

8) $-6x^6y^5$

9) $-24x^9y^6$

10) $-10x^{10}y^5$

11) $-21x^6y^9$

12) $-18x^8y^2$

13) $\frac{1}{125}$

14) $\frac{243}{343}$

15) $3x^2$

16) $\frac{4}{x^2}$

17) $\frac{9}{x^3y^4}$

18) $\frac{xy}{5}$

19) $\frac{1}{4x^4y^2}$

20) $\frac{1}{4x^2y}$

21) $\frac{6}{7y^2}$

22) $\frac{3y^3}{2x^3}$

23) x^6y^6

24) $27x^9y^{12}$

25) $576x^4y^6$

26) $1,000x^3y^9$

27) $\frac{81}{x^4}$

28) $\frac{1}{36y^2}$

29) $\frac{y^3}{512x^6}$

30) $\frac{x^4}{4y^4}$

31) $\frac{x^4y^4}{16}$

32) $\frac{x^2y^2}{16}$

33) 16

34) 9

35) 343

36) $\frac{125}{8}$

37) $\frac{27}{8}$

38) $\frac{625}{81}$

39) $\frac{1}{x^7}$

40) $\frac{3}{y^5}$

41) $\frac{15}{y^3}$

42) $-\frac{20}{x^4}$

43) $\frac{12b^5}{a^3}$

44) $\frac{25a^3}{b^4c^3}$

45) $-\frac{4x^5}{y^3z^6}$

46) $\frac{18y^3}{x^3}$

47) $-\frac{5bc^4}{3a^2}$

48) 4.12×10^{-3}

49) 5.3×10^{-5}

50) 6.6×10^4

51) 7.2×10^7

52) 8

53) 3

54) 13

55) 10

56) 8

57) $9\sqrt{3}$

Effortless Math Education

CHAPTER

7 Expressions and Variables

Math topics that you'll learn in this chapter:

- ☑ Simplifying Variable Expressions
- ☑ Simplifying Polynomial Expressions
- ☑ The Distributive Property
- ☑ Evaluating One Variable
- ☑ Evaluating Two Variables

Simplifying Variable Expressions

- In algebra, a variable is a letter used to stand for a number. The most common letters are $x, y, z, a, b, c, m,$ and n.

- An algebraic expression is an expression that contains integers, variables, and math operations such as addition, subtraction, multiplication, division, etc.

- In an expression, we can combine "like" terms. (values with same variable and same power)

Examples:

Example 1. Simplify. $(4x + 2x + 4) =$

Solution: In this expression, there are three terms: $4x, 2x,$ and 4. Two terms are "like terms": $4x$ and $2x$. Combine like terms. $4x + 2x = 6x$. Then: $(4x + 2x + 4) = 6x + 4$ (***remember you cannot combine variables and numbers.***)

Example 2. Simplify. $-2x^2 - 5x + 4x^2 - 9 =$

Solution: Combine "like" terms: $-2x^2 + 4x^2 = 2x^2$.
Then: $-2x^2 - 5x + 4x^2 - 9 = 2x^2 - 5x - 9$.

Example 3. Simplify. $(-8 + 6x^2 + 3x^2 + 9x) =$

Solution: Combine like terms. Then:
$(-8 + 6x^2 + 3x^2 + 9x) = 9x^2 + 9x - 8$

Example 4. Simplify. $-10x + 6x^2 - 3x + 9x^2 =$

Solution: Combine "like" terms: $-10x - 3x = -13x$, and $6x^2 + 9x^2 = 15x^2$
Then: $-10x + 6x^2 - 3x + 9x^2 = -13x + 15x^2$. Write in standard form (biggest powers first): $-13x + 15x^2 = 15x^2 - 13x$

bit.ly/2WFVudQ

Find more at

Simplifying Polynomial Expressions

- In mathematics, a polynomial is an expression consisting of variables and coefficients that involves only the operations of addition, subtraction, multiplication, and non–negative integer exponents of variables. $P(x) = a_n x^n + a_{n-1} x^{n-1} + \ldots + a_2 x^2 + a_1 x + a_0$

- Polynomials must always be simplified as much as possible. It means you must add together any like terms. (values with same variable and same power)

Examples:

Example 1. Simplify this Polynomial Expressions. $3x^2 - 6x^3 - 2x^3 + 4x^4$

Solution: Combine "like" terms: $-6x^3 - 2x^3 = -8x^3$
Then: $3x^2 - 6x^3 - 2x^3 + 4x^4 = 3x^2 - 8x^3 + 4x^4$
Now, write the expression in standard form: $4x^4 - 8x^3 + 3x^2$

Example 2. Simplify this expression. $(-5x^2 + 2x^3) - (3x^3 - 6x^2) =$

Solution: First, use distributive property: $\rightarrow$ multiply $(-)$ into $(3x^3 - 6x^2)$
$(-5x^2 + 2x^3) - (3x^3 - 6x^2) = -5x^2 + 2x^3 - 3x^3 + 6x^2$
Then combine "like" terms: $-5x^2 + 2x^3 - 3x^3 + 6x^2 = x^2 - x^3$
And write in standard form: $x^2 - x^3 = -x^3 + x^2$

Example 3. Simplify. $3x^3 - 9x^4 - 8x^2 + 12x^4 =$

Solution: Combine "like" terms:
$-9x^4 + 12x^4 = 3x^4$
Then: $3x^3 - 9x^4 - 8x^2 + 12x^4 = 3x^3 + 3x^4 - 8x^2$
And write in standard form: $3x^3 + 3x^4 - 8x^2 = 3x^4 + 3x^3 - 8x^2$

bit.ly/2WT5gtn

Find more at

The Distributive Property

- The distributive property (or the distributive property of multiplication over addition and subtraction) simplifies and solves expressions in the form of: $a(b + c)$ or $a(b - c)$

- The distributive property is multiplying a term outside the parentheses by the terms inside.

- Distributive Property rule: $a(b + c) = ab + ac$

Examples:

Example 1. Simply using the distributive property. $(-2)(x + 3)$

Solution: Use Distributive Property rule: $a(b + c) = ab + ac$
$(-2)(x + 3) = (-2 \times x) + (-2) \times (3) = -2x - 6$

Example 2. Simply. $(-5)(-2x - 6)$

Solution: Use Distributive Property rule: $a(b + c) = ab + ac$
$(-5)(-2x - 6) = (-5 \times -2x) + (-5) \times (-6) = 10x + 30$

Example 3. Simply. $(7)(2x - 8) - 12x$

Solution: First, simplify $(7)(2x - 8)$ using the distributive property.
Then: $(7)(2x - 8) = 14x - 56$
Now combine like terms: $(7)(2x - 8) - 12x = 14x - 56 - 12x$
In this expression, $14x$ and $-12x$ are "like terms" and we can combine them.
$14x - 12x = 2x$. Then: $14x - 56 - 12x = 2x - 56$

Evaluating One Variable

- To evaluate one variable expression, find the variable and substitute a number for that variable.

- Perform the arithmetic operations.

Examples:

Example 1. Calculate this expression for $x = 2$. $8 + 2x$

Solution: First, substitute 2 for x

Then: $8 + 2x = 8 + 2(2)$

Now, use order of operation to find the answer: $8 + 2(2) = 8 + 4 = 12$

Example 2. Evaluate this expression for $x = -1$. $4x - 8$

Solution: First, substitute -1 for x,

Then: $4x - 8 = 4(-1) - 8$

Now, use order of operation to find the answer: $4(-1) - 8 = -4 - 8 = -12$

Example 3. Find the value of this expression when $x = 4$. $16 - 5x$

Solution: First, substitute 4 for x,

Then: $16 - 5x = 16 - 5(4) = 16 - 20 = -4$

Example 4. Solve this expression for $x = -3$. $15 + 7x$

Solution: Substitute -3 for x,

Then: $15 + 7x = 15 + 7(-3) = 15 - 21 = -6$

bit.ly/3ppuiQZ

Find more at

Evaluating Two Variables

- To evaluate an algebraic expression, substitute a number for each variable.

- Perform the arithmetic operations to find the value of the expression.

Examples:

Example 1. Calculate this expression for a = 2 and $b = -1$. $4a - 3b$

Solution: First, substitute 2 for a, and -1 for b ,
*T*hen: $4a - 3b = 4(2) - 3(-1)$
Now, use order of operation to find the answer: $4(2) - 3(-1) = 8 + 3 = 11$

Example 2. Evaluate this expression for $x = -2$ and $y = 2$. $3x + 6y$

Solution: Substitute -2 for x, and 2 for y ,
Then: $3x + 6y = 3(-2) + 6(2) = -6 + 12 = 6$

Example 3. Find the value of this expression $2(6a - 5b)$ when $a = -1$ and $b = 4$.

Solution: Substitute -1 for a, and 4 for b ,
Then: $2(6a - 5b) = 12a - 10b = 12(-1) - 10(4) = -12 - 40 = -52$

Example 4. Solve this expression. $-7x - 2y$, $x = 4$, $y = -3$

Solution: Substitute 4 for x, and -3 for y and simplify.
Then: $-7x - 2y = -7(4) - 2(-3) = -28 + 6 = -22$

Chapter 7: Practices

✍ Simplify each expression.

1) $(3 + 4x - 1) =$

2) $(-5 - 2x + 7) =$

3) $(12x - 5x - 4) =$

4) $(-16x + 24x - 9) =$

5) $(6x + 5 - 15x) =$

6) $2 + 5x - 8x - 6 =$

7) $5x + 10 - 3x - 22 =$

8) $-5 - 3x^2 - 6 + 4x =$

9) $-6 + 9x^2 - 3 + x =$

10) $5x^2 + 3x - 10x - 3 =$

11) $4x^2 - 2x - 6x + 5 - 8 =$

12) $3x^2 - 5x - 7x + 2 - 4 =$

13) $9x^2 - x - 5x + 3 - 9 =$

14) $2x^2 - 7x - 3x^2 + 4x + 6 =$

✍ Simplify each polynomial.

15) $5x^2 + 3x^3 - 9x^2 + 2x = $ _____

16) $8x^4 + 2x^5 - 7x^4 + 3x^2 = $ _____

17) $15x^3 + 11x - 5x^2 - 9x^3 = $ _____

18) $(7x^3 - 3x^2) + (5x^2 - 13x) = $ _____

19) $(12x^4 + 6x^3) + (x^3 - 5x^4) = $ _____

20) $\left(15x^5 - 8x^3\right) - (4x^3 + x^2) = $ _____

21) $(14x^4 + 7x^3) - (x^3 - 24) = $ _____

22) $(20x^4 + 6x^3) - (-x^3 - 2x^4) = $ _____

23) $(x^2 + 9x^3) + (-22x^2 + 6x^3) = $ _____

24) $(4x^4 - 2x^3) + (-5x^3 - 8x^4) = $ _____

Effortless Math Education

✍ Use the distributive property to simply each expression.

25) $2(6 + x) = $ _____

26) $5(3 - 2x) = $ _____

27) $7(1 - 5x) = $ _____

28) $(3 - 4x)7 = $ _____

29) $6(2 - 3x) = $ _____

30) $(-1)(-9 + x) = $ _____

31) $(-6)(3x - 2) = $ _____

32) $(-x + 12)(-4) = $ _____

33) $(-2)(1 - 6x) = $ _____

34) $(-5x - 3)(-8) = $ _____

✍ Evaluate each expression using the value given.

35) $x = 4 \rightarrow 10 - x = $ ____

36) $x = 6 \rightarrow x + 8 = $ ____

37) $x = 3 \rightarrow 2x - 6 = $ ____

38) $x = 2 \rightarrow 10 - 4x = $ ____

39) $x = 7 \rightarrow 8x - 3 = $ ____

40) $x = 9 \rightarrow 20 - 2x = $ ____

41) $x = 5 \rightarrow 10x - 30 = $ ___

42) $x = -6 \rightarrow 5 - x = $ ____

43) $x = -3 \rightarrow 22 - 3x = $ ____

44) $x = -7 \rightarrow 10 - 9x = $ ____

45) $x = -10 \rightarrow 40 - 3x = $ ____

46) $x = -2 \rightarrow 20x - 5 = $ ____

47) $x = -5 \rightarrow -10x - 8 = $ ___

48) $x = -4 \rightarrow -1 - 4x = $ ___

✍ Evaluate each expression using the values given.

49) $x = 2, y = 1 \rightarrow 2x + 7y = $ _____

50) $a = 3, b = 5 \rightarrow 3a - 5b = $ _____

51) $x = 6, y = 2 \rightarrow 3x - 2y + 8 = $ _____

52) $a = -2, b = 3 \rightarrow -5a + 2b + 6 = $ _____

53) $x = -4, y = -3 \rightarrow -4x + 10 - 8y = $ _____

Effortless
Math
Education

Chapter 7: Answers

1) $4x + 2$

2) $-2x + 2$

3) $7x - 4$

4) $8x - 9$

5) $-9x + 5$

6) $-3x - 4$

7) $2x - 12$

8) $-3x^2 + 4x - 11$

9) $9x^2 + x - 9$

10) $5x^2 - 7x - 3$

11) $4x^2 - 8x - 3$

12) $3x^2 - 12x - 2$

13) $9x^2 - 6x - 6$

14) $-x^2 - 3x + 6$

15) $3x^3 - 4x^2 + 2x$

16) $2x^5 + x^4 + 3x^2$

17) $6x^3 - 5x^2 + 11x$

18) $7x^3 + 2x^2 - 13x$

19) $7x^4 + 7x^3$

20) $15x^5 - 12x^3 - x^2$

21) $14x^4 + 6x^3 + 24$

22) $22x^4 + 7x^3$

23) $15x^3 - 21x^2$

24) $-4x^4 - 7x^3$

25) $2x + 12$

26) $-10x + 15$

27) $-35x + 7$

28) $-28x + 21$

29) $-18x + 12$

30) $-x + 9$

31) $-18x + 12$

32) $4x - 48$

33) $12x - 2$

34) $40x + 24$

35) 6

36) 14

37) 0

38) 2

39) 53

40) 2

41) 20

42) 11

43) 31

44) 73

45) 70

46) -45

47) 42

48) 15

49) 11

50) -16

51) 22

52) 22

53) 50

Effortless Math Education

8 Equations and Inequalities

Math topics that you'll learn in this chapter:

- ☑ One-Step Equations
- ☑ Multi-Step Equations
- ☑ System of Equations
- ☑ Graphing Single–Variable Inequalities
- ☑ One-Step Inequalities
- ☑ Multi-Step Inequalities

One–Step Equations

- The values of two expressions on both sides of an equation are equal. Example: $ax = b$. In this equation, ax is equal to b.

- Solving an equation means finding the value of the variable.

- You only need to perform one Math operation to solve the one-step equations.

- To solve a one-step equation, find the inverse (opposite) operation is being performed.

- The inverse operations are:

  ❖ Addition and subtraction
  ❖ Multiplication and division

Examples:

Example 1. Solve this equation for x. $4x = 16, x = ?$

Solution: Here, the operation is multiplication (variable x is multiplied by 4) and its inverse operation is division. To solve this equation, divide both sides of equation by 4: $4x = 16 \rightarrow \frac{4x}{4} = \frac{16}{4} \rightarrow x = 4$

Example 2. Solve this equation. $x + 8 = 0$, $x = ?$

Solution: In this equation 8 is added to the variable x. The inverse operation of addition is subtraction. To solve this equation, subtract 8 from both sides of the equation: $x + 8 - 8 = 0 - 8$. Then: $\rightarrow x = -8$

Example 3. Solve this equation for x. $x - 12 = 0$

Solution: Here, the operation is subtraction and its inverse operation is addition. To solve this equation, add 12 to both sides of the equation:

$$x - 12 + 12 = 0 + 12 \rightarrow x = 12$$

Multi–Step Equations

- To solve a multi-step equation, combine "like" terms on one side.

- Bring variables to one side by adding or subtracting.

- Simplify using the inverse of addition or subtraction.

- Simplify further by using the inverse of multiplication or division.

- Check your solution by plugging the value of the variable into the original equation.

Examples:

Example 1. Solve this equation for x. $4x + 8 = 20 - 2x$

Solution: First, bring variables to one side by adding $2x$ to both sides. Then: $4x + 8 + 2x = 20 - 2x + 2x \rightarrow 4x + 8 + 2x = 20$.

Simplify: $6x + 8 = 20$ Now, subtract 8 from both sides of the equation: $6x + 8 - 8 = 20 - 8 \rightarrow 6x = 12 \rightarrow$ Divide both sides by 6: $6x = 12 \rightarrow \dfrac{6x}{6} = \dfrac{12}{6} \rightarrow x = 2$

Let's check this solution by substituting the value of 2 for x in the original equation:

$x = 2 \rightarrow 4x + 8 = 20 - 2x \rightarrow 4(2) + 8 = 20 - 2(2) \rightarrow 16 = 16$

The answer $x = 2$ is correct.

Example 2. Solve this equation for x. $-5x + 4 = 24$

Solution: Subtract 4 from both sides of the equation.

$-5x + 4 = 24 \rightarrow -5x + 4 - 4 = 24 - 4 \rightarrow -5x = 20$

Divide both sides by -5, then: $-5x = 20 \rightarrow \dfrac{-5x}{-5} = \dfrac{20}{-5} \rightarrow x = -4$

Now, check the solution:

$x = -4 \rightarrow -5x + 4 = 24 \rightarrow -5(-4) + 4 = 24 \rightarrow 24 = 24$

The answer $x = -4$ is correct.

bit.ly/3nQbSEB

Find more at

System of Equations

- A system of equations contains two equations and two variables. For example, consider the system of equations: $x - y = 1, x + y = 5$

- The easiest way to solve a system of equations is using the elimination method. The elimination method uses the addition property of equality. You can add the same value to each side of an equation.

- For the first equation above, you can add $x + y$ to the left side and 5 to the right side of the first equation: $x - y + (x + y) = 1 + 5$. Now, if you simplify, you get: $x - y + (x + y) = 1 + 5 \rightarrow 2x = 6 \rightarrow x = 3$. Now, substitute 3 for the x in the first equation: $3 - y = 1$. By solving this equation, $y = 2$

Example:

Example 1. What is the value of $x + y$ in this system of equations?

$$\begin{cases} 2x + 4y = 12 \\ 4x - 2y = -16 \end{cases}$$

Solution: Solving a System of Equations by Elimination:
Multiply the first equation by (-2), then add it to the second equation.

$$\begin{matrix} -2(2x + 4y = 12) \\ \underline{4x - 2y = -16} \end{matrix} \Rightarrow \begin{matrix} -4x - 8y = -24 \\ 4x - 2y = -16 \end{matrix} \Rightarrow -10y = -40 \Rightarrow y = 4$$

Plug in the value of y into one of the equations and solve for x.
$2x + 4(4) = 12 \Rightarrow 2x + 16 = 12 \Rightarrow 2x = -4 \Rightarrow x = -2$
Thus, $x + y = -2 + 4 = 2$

Graphing Single–Variable Inequalities

- An inequality compares two expressions using an inequality sign.

- Inequality signs are: "less than" <, "greater than" >, "less than or equal to" ≤, and "greater than or equal to" ≥.

- To graph a single–variable inequality, find the value of the inequality on the number line.

- For less than (<) or greater than (>) draw an open circle on the value of the variable. If there is an equal sign too, then use a filled circle.

- Draw an arrow to the right for greater or to the left for less than.

Examples:

Example 1. Draw a graph for this inequality. $x > 2$

Solution: Since the variable is greater than 2, then we need to find 2 in the number line and draw an open circle on it. Then, draw an arrow to the right.

Example 2. Graph this inequality. $x \leq -3$.

Solution: Since the variable is less than or equal to −3, then we need to find −3 in the number line and draw a filled circle on it. Then, draw an arrow to the left.

bit.ly/3aJ4GGo
Find more at

One–Step Inequalities

- An inequality compares two expressions using an inequality sign.

- Inequality signs are: "less than" <, "greater than" >, "less than or equal to" ≤, and "greater than or equal to" ≥.

- You only need to perform one Math operation to solve the one-step inequalities.

- To solve one-step inequalities, find the inverse (opposite) operation is being performed.

- For dividing or multiplying both sides by negative numbers, flip the direction of the inequality sign.

Examples:

Example 1. Solve this inequality for x. $x + 5 \geq 4$

Solution: The inverse (opposite) operation of addition is subtraction. In this inequality, 5 is added to x. To isolate x we need to subtract 5 from both sides of the inequality.
Then: $x + 5 \geq 4 \rightarrow x + 5 - 5 \geq 4 - 5 \rightarrow x \geq -1$. The solution is: $x \geq -1$

Example 2. Solve the inequality. $x - 3 > -6$.

Solution: 3 is subtracted from x. Add 3 to both sides.
$x - 3 > -6 \rightarrow x - 3 + 3 > -6 + 3 \rightarrow x > -3$

Example 3. Solve. $4x \leq -8$.

Solution: 4 is multiplied to x. Divide both sides by 4.
Then: $4x \leq -8 \rightarrow \frac{4x}{4} \leq \frac{-8}{4} \rightarrow x \leq -2$

Example 4. Solve. $-3x \leq 6$.

Solution: -3 is multiplied to x. Divide both sides by -3. Remember when dividing or multiplying both sides of an inequality by negative numbers, flip the direction of the inequality sign.
Then: $-3x \leq 6 \rightarrow \frac{-3x}{-3} \geq \frac{6}{-3} \rightarrow x \geq -2$

bit.ly/3rrElgL

Find more at

Multi−Step Inequalities

- To solve a multi-step inequality, combine "like" terms on one side.

- Bring variables to one side by adding or subtracting.

- Isolate the variable.

- Simplify using the inverse of addition or subtraction.

- Simplify further by using the inverse of multiplication or division.

- For dividing or multiplying both sides by negative numbers, flip the direction of the inequality sign.

Examples:

Example 1. Solve this inequality. $8x - 2 \leq 14$

Solution: In this inequality, 2 is subtracted from $8x$. The inverse of subtraction is addition. Add 2 to both sides of the inequality:

$8x - 2 + 2 \leq 14 + 2 \rightarrow 8x \leq 16$

Now, divide both sides by 8. Then: $8x \leq 16 \rightarrow \frac{8x}{8} \leq \frac{16}{8} \rightarrow x \leq 2$

The solution of this inequality is $x \leq 2$.

Example 2. Solve this inequality. $3x + 9 < 12$

Solution: First, subtract 9 from both sides: $3x + 9 - 9 < 12 - 9$

Then simplify: $3x + 9 - 9 < 12 - 9 \rightarrow 3x < 3$

Now divide both sides by 3: $\frac{3x}{3} < \frac{3}{3} \rightarrow x < 1$

Example 3. Solve this inequality. $-5x + 3 \geq 8$

Solution: First, subtract 3 from both sides:

$-5x + 3 - 3 \geq 8 - 3 \rightarrow -5x \geq 5$

Divide both sides by -5. Remember that you need to flip the direction of inequality sign. $-5x \geq 5 \rightarrow \frac{-5x}{-5} \leq \frac{5}{-5} \rightarrow x \leq -1$

bit.ly/2WK1xOr

Find more at

Chapter 8: Practices

✍ Solve each equation. (One−Step Equations)

1) $x + 6 = 3 \rightarrow x =$ _____ ---

2) $5 = 11 - x \rightarrow x =$ _____

3) $-3 = 8 + x \rightarrow x =$ _____

4) $x - 2 = -7 \rightarrow x =$ _____

5) $-15 = x + 6 \rightarrow x =$ _____

6) $10 - x = -2 \rightarrow x =$ _____

7) $22 - x = -9 \rightarrow x =$ _____

8) $-4 + x = 28 \rightarrow x =$ _____

9) $11 - x = -7 \rightarrow x =$ _____

10) $35 - x = -7 \rightarrow x =$ _____

✍ Solve each equation. (Multi−Step Equations)

11) $4(x + 2) = 12 \rightarrow x =$ _____

12) $-6(6 - x) = 12 \rightarrow x =$ _____

13) $5 = -5(x + 2) \rightarrow x =$ _____

14) $-10 = 2(4 + x) \rightarrow x =$ _____

15) $4(x + 2) = -12, x =$ _____

16) $-6(3 + 2x) = 30, x =$ _____

17) $-3(4 - x) = 12, x =$ _____

18) $-4(6 - x) = 16, x =$ _____

✍ Solve each system of equations.

19) $\begin{cases} x + 6y = 32 \\ x + 3y = 17 \end{cases}$ $x =$ _____ $y =$ _____

20) $\begin{cases} 3x + y = 15 \\ x + 2y = 10 \end{cases}$ $x =$ _____ $y =$ _____

21) $\begin{cases} 3x + 5y = 17 \\ 2x + y = 9 \end{cases}$ $x =$ _____ $y =$ _____

22) $\begin{cases} 5x - 2y = -8 \\ -6x + 2y = 10 \end{cases}$ $x =$ _____ $y =$ _____

Effortless Math Education

✎ **Draw a graph for each inequality.**

23) $x \leq -3$

24) $x > -5$

✎ **Solve each inequality and graph it.**

25) $x - 2 \geq -2$

26) $2x - 3 < 9$

✎ **Solve each inequality.**

27) $x + 13 > 4$ 35) $10 + 5x < -15$

28) $x + 6 > 5$ 36) $6(6 + x) \geq -18$

29) $-12 + 2x \leq 26$ 37) $2(x - 5) \geq -14$

30) $-2 + 8x \leq 14$ 38) $6(x + 4) < -12$

31) $6 + 4x \leq 18$ 39) $3(x - 8) \geq -48$

32) $4(x + 3) \geq -12$ 40) $-(6 - 4x) > -30$

33) $2(6 + x) \geq -12$ 41) $2(2 + 2x) > -60$

34) $3(x - 5) < -6$ 42) $-3(4 + 2x) > -24$

Chapter 8: Answers

1) −3

2) 6

3) −11

4) −5

5) −21

6) 12

7) 31

8) 32

9) 18

10) 42

11) 1

12) 8

13) −3

14) −9

15) −5

16) −4

17) 8

18) 10

19) $x = 2, y = 5$

20) $x = 4, y = 3$

21) $x = 4, y = 1$

22) $x = -2, y = -1$

23) $x \leq -3$

24) $x > -5$

25) $x \geq 0$

26) $x < 6$

27) $x > -9$

28) $x > -1$

29) $x \leq 19$

30) $x \leq 2$

31) $x \leq 3$

32) $x \geq -6$

33) $x \geq -12$

34) $x < 3$

35) $x < -5$

36) $x \geq -9$

37) $x \geq -2$

38) $x < -6$

39) $x \geq -8$

40) $x > -6$

41) $x > -16$

42) $x < 2$

CHAPTER

9 Geometry and Solid Figures

Math topics that you'll learn in this chapter:

- ☑ The Pythagorean Theorem
- ☑ Triangles
- ☑ Polygons
- ☑ Circles
- ☑ Trapezoids
- ☑ Cubes
- ☑ Rectangle Prisms
- ☑ Cylinder

The Pythagorean Theorem

- You can use the Pythagorean Theorem to find a missing side in a right triangle.

- In any right triangle: $a^2 + b^2 = c^2$

Examples:

Example 4. Right triangle ABC (not shown) has two legs of lengths 3 cm (AB) and 4 cm (AC). What is the length of the hypotenuse of the triangle (side BC)?

Solution: Use Pythagorean Theorem: $a^2 + b^2 = c^2$, $a = 3$, and $b = 4$
Then: $a^2 + b^2 = c^2 \rightarrow 3^2 + 4^2 = c^2 \rightarrow 9 + 16 = c^2 \rightarrow 25 = c^2 \rightarrow c = \sqrt{25} = 5$
The length of the hypotenuse is 5 cm.

Example 5. Find the hypotenuse of this triangle.

Solution: Use Pythagorean Theorem: $a^2 + b^2 = c^2$
Then: $a^2 + b^2 = c^2 \rightarrow 8^2 + 6^2 = c^2 \rightarrow 64 + 36 = c^2$
$c^2 = 100 \rightarrow c = \sqrt{100} = 10$

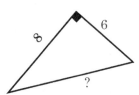

Example 6. Find the length of the missing side in this triangle.

Solution: Use Pythagorean Theorem: $a^2 + b^2 = c^2$
Then: $a^2 + b^2 = c^2 \rightarrow 12^2 + b^2 = 15^2 \rightarrow 144 + b^2 = 225 \rightarrow$
$b^2 = 225 - 144 \rightarrow b^2 = 81 \rightarrow b = \sqrt{81} = 9$

Triangles

- In any triangle, the sum of all angles is 180 degrees.

- Area of a triangle $= \frac{1}{2} (base \times height)$

Examples:

What is the area of the following triangles?

Example 1.

Solution: Use the area formula:
Area $= \frac{1}{2} (base \times height)$
$base = 14$ and $height = 10$
Area $= \frac{1}{2}(14 \times 10) = \frac{1}{2}(140) = 70$

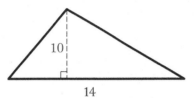

Example 2.

Solution: Use the area formula:
Area $= \frac{1}{2} (base \times height)$
$base = 16$ and $height = 8$; Area $= \frac{1}{2}(16 \times 8) = \frac{128}{2} = 64$

Example 3. What is the missing angle in this triangle?

Solution:
In any triangle, the sum of all angles is 180 degrees.
Let x be the missing angle.
Then: $55 + 80 + x = 180$;
$\rightarrow 135 + x = 180 \rightarrow x = 180 - 135 = 45$
The missing angle is 45 degrees.

bit.ly/3haZrRg

Find more at

Polygons

- The perimeter of a square = $4 \times side = 4s$

- The perimeter of a rectangle= $2(width + length)$

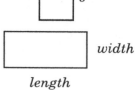

- The perimeter of trapezoid= $a + b + c + d$

- The perimeter of a regular hexagon = $6a$

- The perimeter of a parallelogram = $2(l + w)$

Examples:

Example 1. Find the perimeter of following regular hexagon.

Solution: Since the hexagon is regular, all sides are equal.
Then: The perimeter of The hexagon = $6 \times (one\ side)$
The perimeter of The hexagon = $6 \times (one\ side) = 6 \times 8 = 48\ m$

Example 2. Find the perimeter of following trapezoid.

Solution: The perimeter of a trapezoid = $a + b + c + d$
The perimeter of the trapezoid = $7 + 8 + 8 + 10 = 33\ ft$

Circles

- In a circle, variable r is usually used for the radius and d for diameter.

- *Area of a circle* $= \pi r^2$ (π is about 3.14)

- *Circumference of a circle* $= 2\pi r$

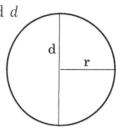

Examples:

Example 1. Find the area of this circle.

Solution:
Use area formula: $Area = \pi r^2$
$r = 6\ in \rightarrow Area = \pi(6)^2 = 36\pi$, $\pi = 3.14$
Then: $Area = 36 \times 3.14 = 113.04\ in^2$

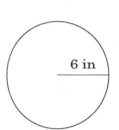

Example 2. Find the Circumference of this circle.

Solution:
Use Circumference formula: $Circumference = 2\pi r$
$r = 8\ cm \rightarrow Circumference = 2\pi(8) = 16\pi$
$\pi = 3.14$ Then: $Circumference = 16 \times 3.14 = 50.24\ cm$

Example 3. Find the area of the circle.

Solution:
Use area formula: $Area = \pi r^2$,
$r = 9\ in$ then: $Area = \pi(9)^2 = 81\pi$, $\pi = 3.14$
Then: $Area = 81 \times 3.14 = 254.34\ in^2$

bit.ly/3nJdOP2
Find more at

Trapezoids

- A quadrilateral with at least one pair of parallel sides is a trapezoid.

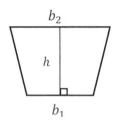

- Area of a trapezoid $= \frac{1}{2}h(b_1 + b_2)$

Examples:

Example 1. Calculate the area of this trapezoid.

Solution:

Use area formula: $A = \frac{1}{2}h(b_1 + b_2)$

$b_1 = 6\ cm$, $b_2 = 10\ cm$ and $h = 12\ cm$

Then: $A = \frac{1}{2}(12)(10 + 6) = 6(16) = 96\ cm^2$

Example 2. Calculate the area of this trapezoid.

Solution:

Use area formula: $A = \frac{1}{2}h(b_1 + b_2)$

$b_1 = 10\ cm$, $b_2 = 18\ cm$ and $h = 14\ cm$

Then: $A = \frac{1}{2}(14)(10 + 18) = 7(28) = 196\ cm^2$

Cubes

- A cube is a three-dimensional solid object bounded by six square sides.

- Volume is the measure of the amount of space inside of a solid figure, like a cube, ball, cylinder or pyramid.

- The volume of a cube = $(one\ side)^3$

- The surface area of a cube = $6 \times (one\ side)^2$

Examples:

Example 1. Find the volume and surface area of this cube.

Solution: Use volume formula: $volume = (one\ side)^3$
Then: $volume = (one\ side)^3 = (3)^3 = 27\ cm^3$
Use surface area formula:
$surface\ area\ of\ cube: 6(one\ side)^2 = 6(3)^2 = 6(9) = 54\ cm^2$

Example 2. Find the volume and surface area of this cube.

Solution: Use volume formula: $volume = (one\ side)^3$
Then: $volume = (one\ side)^3 = (6)^3 = 216\ cm^3$
Use surface area formula:
$surface\ area\ of\ cube: 6(one\ side)^2 = 6(6)^2 = 6(36) = 216\ cm^2$

Example 3. Find the volume and surface area of this cube.

Solution: Use volume formula: $volume = (one\ side)^3$
Then: $volume = (one\ side)^3 = (8)^3 = 512\ m^3$
Use surface area formula:
$surface\ area\ of\ cube: 6(one\ side)^2 = 6(8)^2 = 6(64) = 384\ m^2$

bit.ly/2M6PfOl

Find more at

Rectangular Prisms

- A rectangular prism is a solid 3-dimensional object with six rectangular faces.

- The volume of a Rectangular prism $= Length \times Width \times Height$

$Volume = l \times w \times h$

$Surface\ area = 2 \times (wh + lw + lh)$

Examples:

Example 1. Find the volume and surface area of this rectangular prism.

Solution: Use volume formula: $Volume = l \times w \times h$

Then: $Volume = 7 \times 5 \times 9 = 315\ m^3$

Use surface area formula: $Surface\ area = 2 \times (wh + lw + lh)$

Then: $Surface\ area = 2 \times \big((5 \times 9) + (7 \times 5) + (7 \times 9)\big)$

$\qquad = 2 \times (45 + 35 + 63) = 2 \times (143) = 286\ m^2$

Example 2. Find the volume and surface area of this rectangular prism.

Solution: Use volume formula: $Volume = l \times w \times h$

Then: $Volume = 9 \times 6 \times 12 = 648\ m^3$

Use surface area formula: $Surface\ area = 2 \times (wh + lw + lh)$

Then: $Surface\ area = 2 \times \big((6 \times 12) + (9 \times 6) + (9 \times 12)\big)$

$\qquad = 2 \times (72 + 54 + 108) = 2 \times (234) = 468\ m^2$

Cylinder

- A cylinder is a solid geometric figure with straight parallel sides and a circular or oval cross-section.

- *Volume of a Cylinder* $= \pi(radius)^2 \times height$, $\pi \approx 3.14$

- *Surface area of a cylinder* $= 2\pi r^2 + 2\pi rh$

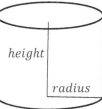

Examples:

Example 1. Find the volume and Surface area of the follow Cylinder.

Solution: Use volume formula:

$Volume = \pi(radius)^2 \times height$

Then: $Volume = \pi(4)^2 \times 10 = 16\pi \times 10 = 160\pi$

$\pi = 3.14$ then: $Volume = 160\pi = 160 \times 3.14 = 502.4 \; cm^3$

Use surface area formula: $Surface \; area = 2\pi r^2 + 2\pi rh$

Then: $2\pi(4)^2 + 2\pi(4)(10) = 2\pi(16) + 2\pi(40) = 32\pi + 80\pi = 112\pi$

$\pi = 3.14$ Then: $Surface \; area = 112 \times 3.14 = 351.68 \; cm^2$

Example 2. Find the volume and Surface area of the follow Cylinder.

Solution: Use volume formula:

$Volume = \pi(radius)^2 \times height$

Then: $Volume = \pi(5)^2 \times 8 = \pi 25 \times 8 = 200\pi$

$\pi = 3.14$ then: $Volume = 200\pi = 628 \; cm^3$

Use surface area formula: $Surface \; area = 2\pi r^2 + 2\pi rh$

Then: $= 2\pi(5)^2 + 2\pi(5)(8) = 2\pi(25) + 2\pi(40) = 50\pi + 80\pi = 130\pi$

$\pi = 3.14$ then: $Surface \; area = 130 \times 3.14 = 408.2 \; cm^2$

bit.ly/37LtcVM

Find more at

Chapter 9: Practices

✎ Find the missing side?

1)

2)

3)

4)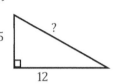

✎ Find the measure of the unknown angle in each triangle.

5)

6)

7)

8)

✎ Find the area of each triangle.

9)

10)

11)

12)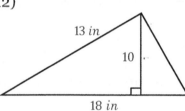

✎ Find the perimeter or circumference of each shape.

13)

14)

15)

16) *regular hexagon*

✎ **Find the area of each trapezoid.**

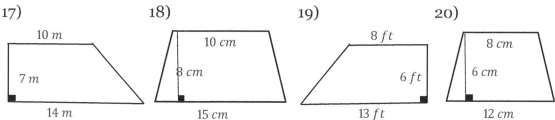

17)   18)   19)   20)

10 m   10 cm   8 ft   8 cm
7 m   8 cm   6 ft   6 cm
14 m   15 cm   13 ft   12 cm

✎ **Find the volume of each cube.**

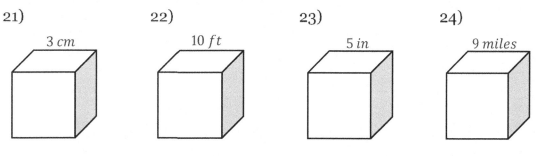

21)   22)   23)   24)

3 cm   10 ft   5 in   9 miles

✎ **Find the volume of each Rectangular Prism.**

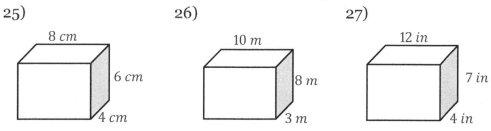

25)   26)   27)

8 cm   10 m   12 in
6 cm   8 m   7 in
4 cm   3 m   4 in

✎ **Find the volume of each Cylinder. Round your answer to the nearest tenth. ($\pi = 3.14$)**

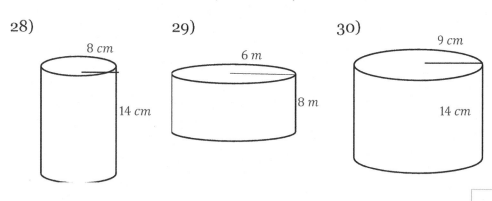

28)   29)   30)

8 cm   6 m   9 cm
14 cm   8 m   14 cm

Effortless
Math
Education

Chapter 9: Answers

1) 4

2) 15

3) 6

4) 13

5) 50

6) 76

7) 84

8) 70

9) 30

10) 49.5

11) 64 cm^2

12) 90 in^2

13) 44 cm

14) 30 ft

15) 10 π ≈ 31.4 in

16) 24 m

17) 84 m^2

18) 100 cm^2

19) 63 ft^2

20) 60 cm^2

21) 27 cm^3

22) 1,000 ft^3

23) 125 in^3

24) 729 mi^3

25) 192 cm^3

26) 240 m^3

27) 336 in^3

28) 2,813.44 cm^3

29) 904.32 m^3

30) 3,560.76 cm^3

CHAPTER

10 **Statistics**

Math topics that you'll learn in this chapter:

- ☑ Mean, Median, Mode, and Range of the Given Data
- ☑ Pie Graph
- ☑ Probability Problems
- ☑ Permutations and Combinations

Mean, Median, Mode, and Range of the Given Data

- Mean: $\dfrac{\textit{sum of the data}}{\textit{total number of data entires}}$

- Mode: the value in the list that appears most often

- Median: is the middle number of a group of numbers arranged in order by size.

- Range: the difference of the largest value and smallest value in the list

Examples:

Example 1. What is the mode of these numbers? $5, 6, 8, 6, 8, 5, 3, 5$

Solution: Mode: the value in the list that appears most often.
Therefore, the mode is number 5. There are three number 5 in the data.

Example 2. What is the median of these numbers? $6, 11, 15, 10, 17, 20, 7$

Solution: Write the numbers in order: $6, 7, 10, 11, 15, 17, 20$
The median is the number in the middle. Therefore, the median is 11.

Example 3. What is the mean of these numbers? $7, 2, 3, 2, 4, 8, 7, 5$

Solution: Mean: $\dfrac{\textit{sum of the data}}{\textit{total number of data entires}} = \dfrac{7+2+3+2+4+8+7+5}{8} = \dfrac{38}{8} = 4.75$

Example 4. What is the range in this list? $3, 7, 12, 6, 15, 20, 8$

Solution: Range is the difference of the largest value and smallest value in the list. The largest value is 20 and the smallest value is 3.
Then: $20 - 3 = 17$

Pie Graph

- A Pie Chart is a circle chart divided into sectors, each sector represents the relative size of each value.

- Pie charts represent a snapshot of how a group is broken down into smaller pieces.

Example:

A library has 750 books that include Mathematics, Physics, Chemistry, English and History. Use the following graph to answer the questions.

Example 1. What is the number of Mathematics books?

Solution: Number of total books = 750

Percent of Mathematics books = 28% = 0.28

Then, the number of Mathematics books: $0.28 \times 750 = 210$

Example 2. What is the number of History books?

Solution: Number of total books = 750

Percent of History books = 12% = 0.12

Then: $0.12 \times 750 = 90$

Example 3. What is the number of Chemistry books?

Solution: Number of total books = 750

Percent of Chemistry books = 22% = 0.22

Then: $0.22 \times 750 = 165$

Probability Problems

- Probability is the likelihood of something happening in the future. It is expressed as a number between zero (can never happen) to 1 (will always happen).

- Probability can be expressed as a fraction, a decimal, or a percent.

- Probability formula: $Probability = \frac{number\ of\ desired\ outcomes}{number\ of\ total\ outcomes}$

Examples:

Example 1. Anita's trick–or–treat bag contains 10 pieces of chocolate, 16 suckers, 16 pieces of gum, 22 pieces of licorice. If she randomly pulls a piece of candy from her bag, what is the probability of her pulling out a piece of sucker?

Solution: Probability $= \frac{number\ of\ desired\ outcomes}{number\ of\ total\ outcomes}$

Probability of pulling out a piece of sucker $= \dfrac{16}{10 + 16 + 16 + 22} = \dfrac{16}{64} = \dfrac{1}{4}$

Example 2. A bag contains 20 balls: four green, five black, eight blue, a brown, a red and one white. If 19 balls are removed from the bag at random, what is the probability that a brown ball has been removed?

Solution: If 19 balls are removed from the bag at random, there will be one ball in the bag. The probability of choosing a brown ball is 1 out of 20. Therefore, the probability of not choosing a brown ball is 19 out of 20 and the probability of having not a brown ball after removing 19 balls is the same. The answer is: $\frac{19}{20}$

Permutations and Combinations

Factorials are products, indicated by an exclamation mark. For example, $4! = 4 \times 3 \times 2 \times 1$ (Remember that $0!$ is defined to be equal to 1)

- **Permutations:** The number of ways to choose a sample of k elements from a set of n distinct objects where order does matter, and replacements are not allowed. For a permutation problem, use this formula:

$$_n\mathrm{P}_k = \frac{n!}{(n-k)!}$$

- **Combination:** The number of ways to choose a sample of r elements from a set of n distinct objects where order does not matter, and replacements are not allowed. For a combination problem, use this formula:

$$_n\mathrm{C}_r = \frac{n!}{r!\,(n-r)!}$$

Examples:

Example 1. How many ways can the first and second place be awarded to 7 people?

Solution: Since the order matters, (the first and second place are different!) we need to use permutation formula where n is 7 and k is 2. Then: $\frac{n!}{(n-k)!} = \frac{7!}{(7-2)!} = \frac{7!}{5!} = \frac{7 \times 6 \times 5!}{5!}$, remove $5!$ from both sides of the fraction. Then: $\frac{7 \times 6 \times 5!}{5!} = 7 \times 6 = 42$

Example 2. How many ways can we pick a team of 3 people from a group of 8?

Solution: Since the order doesn't matter, we need to use a combination formula where n is 8 and r is 3.

Then: $\frac{n!}{r!\,(n-r)!} = \frac{8!}{3!\,(8-3)!} = \frac{8!}{3!\,(5)!} = \frac{8 \times 7 \times 6 \times 5!}{3!\,(5)!} = \frac{8 \times 7 \times 6}{3 \times 2 \times 1} = \frac{336}{6} = 56$

Chapter 10: Practices

✎ Find the values of the Given Data.

1) 6, 11, 5, 3, 6

Mode: _____   Range: _____

Mean: _____   Median: _____

2) 4, 9, 1, 9, 6, 7

Mode: _____   Range: _____

Mean: _____   Median: _____

3) 10, 3, 6, 10, 4, 15

Mode: _____   Range: _____

Mean: _____   Median: _____

4) 12, 4, 8, 9, 3, 12, 15

Mode: _____   Range: _____

Mean: _____   Median: _____

✎ The circle graph below shows all Bob's expenses for last month. Bob spent $790 on his Rent last month.

5) How much did Bob's total expenses last month? _____

6) How much did Bob spend for foods last month? _____

7) How much did Bob spend for his bills last month? _____

8) How much did Bob spend on his car last month? _____

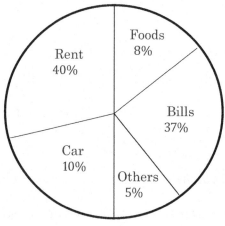

Bob's last month expenses

Rent 40%

Foods 8%

Bills 37%

Others 5%

Car 10%

Effortless Math Education

✎ **Solve.**

9) Bag A contains 8 red marbles and 6 green marbles. Bag B contains 5 black marbles and 7 orange marbles. What is the probability of selecting a green marble at random from bag A? What is the probability of selecting a black marble at random from Bag B?

_____   _____

✎ **Solve.**

10) Susan is baking cookies. She uses sugar, flour, butter, and eggs. How many different orders of ingredients can she try? _____

11) Jason is planning for his vacation. He wants to go to museum, go to the beach, and play volleyball. How many different ways of ordering are there for him? _____

12) In how many ways can a team of 6 basketball players choose a captain and co-captain? _____

13) How many ways can you give 5 balls to your 8 friends? _____

14) A professor is going to arrange her 5 students in a straight line. In how many ways can she do this? _____

15) In how many ways can a teacher chooses 12 out of 15 students?

_____

Effortless
Math
Education

Chapter 10: Answers

1) Mode: 6, Range: 8, Mean: 6.2, Median: 6

2) Mode: 9, Range:8, Mean: 6, Median: 6.5

3) Mode: 10, Range: 12, Mean: 8, Median: 8

4) Mode: 12, Range: 12, Mean: 9, Median: 9

5) $1,975

6) $158

7) $730.75

8) $197.50

9) $\frac{3}{7}, \frac{5}{12}$

10) 24

11) 6

12) 30 (it's a permutation problem)

13) 56 (it's a combination problem)

14) 120

15) 455 (it's a combination problem)

Time to Test

Time to refine your skill with a practice examination

Take a practice SSAT Middle Level Mathematics Test to simulate the test day experience. After you've finished, score your test using the answer keys.

Before You Start

- You'll need a pencil and a timer to take the test.

- After you've finished the test, review the answer key to see where you went wrong.

- Use the answer sheet provided to record your answers. (You can cut it out or photocopy it)

- You will receive 1 point for every correct answer, and you will lose $\frac{1}{4}$ point for each incorrect answer. There is no penalty for skipping a question.

Calculators are NOT permitted for the SSAT Middle Level Test

SSAT Middle Level Math Practice Test 1

2023 - 2023

Two Parts

Total number of questions: 50

Section 1: 25 questions

Section 2: 25 questions

Total time for two parts: 60 Minutes

SSAT Middle Level Math Practice Test 1 Answer Sheet

Remove (or photocopy) this answer sheet and use it to complete the practice test.

SSAT Middle Level Mathematics Practice Test 1 Answer Sheet

SSAT Middle Level Practice Test 1 Section 1

1	Ⓐ Ⓑ Ⓒ Ⓓ Ⓔ	11	Ⓐ Ⓑ Ⓒ Ⓓ Ⓔ	21 Ⓐ Ⓑ Ⓒ Ⓓ Ⓔ
2	Ⓐ Ⓑ Ⓒ Ⓓ Ⓔ	12	Ⓐ Ⓑ Ⓒ Ⓓ Ⓔ	22 Ⓐ Ⓑ Ⓒ Ⓓ Ⓔ
3	Ⓐ Ⓑ Ⓒ Ⓓ Ⓔ	13	Ⓐ Ⓑ Ⓒ Ⓓ Ⓔ	23 Ⓐ Ⓑ Ⓒ Ⓓ Ⓔ
4	Ⓐ Ⓑ Ⓒ Ⓓ Ⓔ	14	Ⓐ Ⓑ Ⓒ Ⓓ Ⓔ	24 Ⓐ Ⓑ Ⓒ Ⓓ Ⓔ
5	Ⓐ Ⓑ Ⓒ Ⓓ Ⓔ	15	Ⓐ Ⓑ Ⓒ Ⓓ Ⓔ	25 Ⓐ Ⓑ Ⓒ Ⓓ Ⓔ
6	Ⓐ Ⓑ Ⓒ Ⓓ Ⓔ	16	Ⓐ Ⓑ Ⓒ Ⓓ Ⓔ	
7	Ⓐ Ⓑ Ⓒ Ⓓ Ⓔ	17	Ⓐ Ⓑ Ⓒ Ⓓ Ⓔ	
8	Ⓐ Ⓑ Ⓒ Ⓓ Ⓔ	18	Ⓐ Ⓑ Ⓒ Ⓓ Ⓔ	
9	Ⓐ Ⓑ Ⓒ Ⓓ Ⓔ	19	Ⓐ Ⓑ Ⓒ Ⓓ Ⓔ	
10	Ⓐ Ⓑ Ⓒ Ⓓ Ⓔ	20	Ⓐ Ⓑ Ⓒ Ⓓ Ⓔ	

SSAT Middle Level Practice Test 1 Section 2

1	Ⓐ Ⓑ Ⓒ Ⓓ Ⓔ	11	Ⓐ Ⓑ Ⓒ Ⓓ Ⓔ	21 Ⓐ Ⓑ Ⓒ Ⓓ Ⓔ
2	Ⓐ Ⓑ Ⓒ Ⓓ Ⓔ	12	Ⓐ Ⓑ Ⓒ Ⓓ Ⓔ	22 Ⓐ Ⓑ Ⓒ Ⓓ Ⓔ
3	Ⓐ Ⓑ Ⓒ Ⓓ Ⓔ	13	Ⓐ Ⓑ Ⓒ Ⓓ Ⓔ	23 Ⓐ Ⓑ Ⓒ Ⓓ Ⓔ
4	Ⓐ Ⓑ Ⓒ Ⓓ Ⓔ	14	Ⓐ Ⓑ Ⓒ Ⓓ Ⓔ	24 Ⓐ Ⓑ Ⓒ Ⓓ Ⓔ
5	Ⓐ Ⓑ Ⓒ Ⓓ Ⓔ	15	Ⓐ Ⓑ Ⓒ Ⓓ Ⓔ	25 Ⓐ Ⓑ Ⓒ Ⓓ Ⓔ
6	Ⓐ Ⓑ Ⓒ Ⓓ Ⓔ	16	Ⓐ Ⓑ Ⓒ Ⓓ Ⓔ	
7	Ⓐ Ⓑ Ⓒ Ⓓ Ⓔ	17	Ⓐ Ⓑ Ⓒ Ⓓ Ⓔ	
8	Ⓐ Ⓑ Ⓒ Ⓓ Ⓔ	18	Ⓐ Ⓑ Ⓒ Ⓓ Ⓔ	
9	Ⓐ Ⓑ Ⓒ Ⓓ Ⓔ	19	Ⓐ Ⓑ Ⓒ Ⓓ Ⓔ	
10	Ⓐ Ⓑ Ⓒ Ⓓ Ⓔ	20	Ⓐ Ⓑ Ⓒ Ⓓ Ⓔ	

SSAT Middle Level Math

Practice Test 1

Section 1

25 questions

Total time for this test: 30 Minutes

You may NOT use a calculator on this part.

1. If 30 percent of a number is 60, then 20 percent of the same number is ...
   (A) 12
   (B) 18
   (C) 25
   (D) 30
   (E) 40

2. Which of the following is NOT equal to 2×0.4?
   (A) 4×0.2
   (B) 1×0.8
   (C) $\frac{16}{8} \times \frac{4}{10}$
   (D) $\frac{5}{15} \times 3$
   (E) 0.8×1

3. Sara has M books. Mary has 6 more books than Sara. If Mary gives Sara 4 books, how many books will Mary have, in terms of M?
   (A) M
   (B) $M + 1$
   (C) $M + 2$
   (D) $M + 6$
   (E) $M - 6$

4. If $\frac{x}{2} = 30$, then $\frac{3x}{2} =$?
   (A) 10
   (B) 20
   (C) 30
   (D) 45
   (E) 90

5. Which of the following is closest to $\frac{1}{6}$ of 40?
   (A) 0.3×6
   (B) 0.3×5
   (C) 0.2×30
   (D) 0.2×35
   (E) 0.2×39.5

6. What is the area of a square whose diagonal is 8?
   (A) 16
   (B) 32
   (C) 36
   (D) 64
   (E) 80

7. An angle is equal to one fifth of its supplement. What is the measure of that angle?
   (A) 20
   (B) 30
   (C) 45
   (D) 60
   (E) 150

8. A $44 shirt now selling for $28 is discounted by approximately what percent?
   (A) 20%
   (B) 36%
   (C) 40%
   (D) 60%
   (E) 80%

9. 6 liters of water are poured into an aquarium that's $25 cm$ long, $5 cm$ wide, and $60 cm$ high. How many centimeters will the water level in the aquarium rise due to this added water? ($1 \ liter \ of \ water = 1,000 \ cm^3$)
   (A) 80
   (B) 48
   (C) 20
   (D) 10
   (E) 8

10. The perimeter of the trapezoid below (not drawn to scale) is 56. What is its area?
    (A) $260 \ cm^2$
    (B) $234 \ cm^2$
    (C) $216 \ cm^2$
    (D) $180 \ cm^2$
    (E) $108 \ cm^2$

17 cm

8 cm

16 cm

11. The score of Emma was half as that of Ava and the score of Mia was twice that of Ava. If the score of Mia was 40, what is the score of Emma?
   (A) 10
   (B) 18
   (C) 20
   (D) 30
   (E) 32

12. Two third of 9 is equal to $\frac{2}{5}$ of what number?
   (A) 60
   (B) 20
   (C) 15
   (D) 30
   (E) 36

13. If three times a number added to 5 equals to 32, what is the number?
   (A) 2
   (B) 4
   (C) 6
   (D) 9
   (E) 10

14. Solve for x: $4(x + 1) = 6(x - 4) + 20$
   (A) 12
   (B) 6.5
   (C) 4
   (D) 2
   (E) 1

15. Karen is 9 years older than her sister Michelle, and Michelle is 4 years younger than her brother David. If the sum of their ages is 82, how old is Michelle?

   (A) 14
   (B) 23
   (C) 22
   (D) 25
   (E) 30

Type equation here.

16. Two-kilograms apple and two-kilograms orange cost \$26.4. If one-kilogram apple costs \$4.2 how much does one-kilogram orange cost?
(A) \$9
(B) \$6
(C) \$5.5
(D) \$5
(E) \$4.5

17. The average weight of 18 girls in a class is 50 kg and the average weight of 32 boys in the same class is 62 kg. What is the average weight of all the 50 students in that class?
(A) 57.68
(B) 61.68
(C) 61.90
(D) 62.20
(E) 64.00

18. What is the value of x in this equation? $6(x + 4) = 78$
(A) 4
(B) 6
(C) 9
(D) 10
(E) 12

19. When a number is subtracted from 32 and the difference is divided by that number, the result is 3. What is the value of the number?

(A)   2
(B)   4
(C)   8
(D)   12
(E)   15

20. Which is the correct statement?
(A) $\frac{3}{4} > 0.8$
(B) $10\% = \frac{2}{5}$
(C) $3 < \frac{5}{2}$
(D) $\frac{5}{6} > 0.8$
(E) $2.5\% = 0.25$

21. In a group of 5 books, the average number of pages is 24. Mary adds a book with 36 pages to the group. What is the new average number of pages per book?
    (A) 20
    (B) 22
    (C) 24
    (D) 26
    (E) 30

22. A football team won exactly 70% of the games it played during last session. Which of the following could be the total number of games the team played last season?
    (A) 49
    (B) 40
    (C) 32
    (D) 12
    (E) 9

23. If a gas tank can hold 35 gallons, how many gallons does it contain when it is $\frac{2}{5}$ full?
    (A) 50
    (B) 125
    (C) 62.5
    (D) 14
    (E) 8

24. What is the value of x in the following figure? (Figure is not drawn to scale)
    (A) 150
    (B) 145
    (C) 125
    (D) 105
    (E) 85

25. The capacity of a red box is 20% bigger than the capacity of a blue box. If 36 books can be put in the red box, how many books can be put in the blue box?

    (A) 15
    (B) 20
    (C) 24
    (D) 30
    (E) 32

IF YOU FINISH BEFORE TIME IS CALLED, YOU MAY CHECK YOUR WORK ON THIS SECTION ONLY. DO NOT TURN TO OTHER SECTION IN THE TEST. | **STOP**

SSAT Middle Level Math

Practice Test 1

Section 2

25 questions

Total time for this test: 30 Minutes

You may NOT use a calculator on this part.

1. A taxi driver earns $8 per 1-hour work. If he works 10 hours a day and in 1 hour he uses 2-liters petrol with price $1 for 1-liter. How much money does he earn in one day?
   (A) $90
   (B) $88
   (C) $70
   (D) $60
   (E) $56

2. Which of the following is less than $\frac{1}{5}$?
   (A) $\frac{1}{4}$
   (B) 0.5
   (C) $\frac{1}{7}$
   (D) 0.28
   (E) 0.31

3. Amy and John work in a same company. Last month, both of them received a raise of 20 percent. If Amy earns $30.00 per hour now and John earns $28.80, Amy earned how much more per hour than John before their raises?
   (A) $8.25
   (B) $4.25
   (C) $3.00
   (D) $2.25
   (E) $1.00

4. Three people can paint 3 houses in 12 days. How many people are needed to paint 6 houses in 6 days?
   (A) 6
   (B) 8
   (C) 12
   (D) 16
   (E) 20

5. If $N \times (6 - 3) = 12$ then $N =$?
   (A) 4
   (B) 12
   (C) 13
   (D) 14
   (E) 18

6. The length of a rectangle is 3 times of its width. If the length is 24, what is the perimeter of the rectangle?
   (A) 24
   (B) 30
   (C) 36
   (D) 48
   (E) 64

7. In the figure below, what is the value of x? (Figure is not drawn to scale)
   (A) 43
   (B) 72
   (C) 77
   (D) 90
   (E) 98

8. If $x \blacksquare y = 4x + y - 2$, what is the value of $4 \blacksquare 12$?
   (A) 4
   (B) 18
   (C) 26
   (D) 36
   (E) 48

9. The width of a rectangle is $4x$, the length is $6x$, and the perimeter of the rectangle is 90. What is the value of x?
   (A) 1
   (B) 2.2
   (C) 3
   (D) 4.5
   (E) 5.8

10. How many tiles of $8\ cm^2$ is needed to cover a floor of dimension $7\ cm$ by $24\ cm$?
    (A) 6
    (B) 12
    (C) 21
    (D) 24
    (E) 30

11. If 0.65 equals $65M$, what is the value of M?
   (A) 0.10
   (B) 0.01
   (C) 1.00
   (D) 11.01
   (E) 0.11

12. If $z = 3x + 5$, what does $2z + 3$ equal?
   (A) $6x + 6$
   (B) $6x + 12$
   (C) $6x - 12$
   (D) $6x - 6$
   (E) $6x + 13$

13. If 96 is the product of 4 and $8x$, then 96 is divisible by which of the following?
   (A) $x + 4$
   (B) $2x - 1$
   (C) $5x - 3$
   (D) $x \times 3$
   (E) $3x + 1$

$$0.0ABC \qquad\qquad\qquad 0.0D$$

14. The letters represent two decimals listed above. One of the decimals is equivalent to $\frac{1}{16}$ and the other is equivalent to $\frac{1}{25}$. What is the product of C and D?
   (A) 0
   (B) 5
   (C) 25
   (D) 20
   (E) 40

15. $\frac{x}{x-2} = \frac{4}{5}$, $x - 5 =$?
   (A) -13
   (B) -15
   (C) -17
   (D) 12
   (E) 15

16. A company pays its employer $7,000 plus 3% of all sales profit. If x is the number of all sales profit, which of the following represents the employer's revenue?

   (A) $0.03x$
   (B) $0.97x - 7,000$
   (C) $0.03x + 7,000$
   (D) $0.97x + 7,000$
   (E) $0.3x + 7,000$

17. In a certain bookshelf of a library, there are 35 biology books, 85 history books, and 90 language books. What is the ratio of the number of biology books to the total number of books in this bookshelf?

   (A) $\frac{1}{4}$
   (B) $\frac{1}{6}$
   (C) $\frac{2}{7}$
   (D) $\frac{3}{8}$
   (E) $\frac{1}{4}$

18. If $5,000 + A - 200 = 7,400$, then $A = \cdots$
   (A) 200
   (B) 600
   (C) 1,600
   (D) 2,600
   (E) 3,000

19. The circle graph below shows all Mr. Green's expenses for last month. If he spent $770 on his car, how much did he spend for his rent?
   (A) $700
   (B) $740
   (C) $780
   (D) $810
   (E) $945

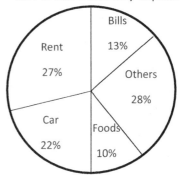

Mr. Green's monthly expenses

20. If $5 \times M + 3 = 5$, M equals to ....
   (A) 2
   (B) 4
   (C) $\frac{2}{5}$
   (D) 6
   (E) $\frac{1}{3}$

21. Which of the following is equal to $\frac{52.6}{100}$?
   (A) 52.6
   (B) 5.26
   (C) 526.0
   (D) 0.0526
   (E) 0.526

22. In the following figure, point Q lies on line A, what is the value of y if $x = 28$? (Figure is not drawn to scale)
   (A) 32
   (B) 37
   (C) 42
   (D) 45
   (E) 56

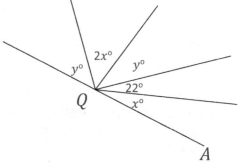

23. A container holds 2.5 gallons of water when it is $\frac{5}{24}$ full. How many gallons of water does the container hold when it's full?
   (A) 8
   (B) 12
   (C) 16
   (D) 20
   (E) 30

24. At a Zoo, the ratio of lions to tigers is 3 to 1. Which of the following could NOT be the total number of lions and tigers in the zoo?
   (A) 64
   (B) 80
   (C) 98
   (D) 104
   (E) 160

25. If x is greater than 18, then $\frac{1}{3}$ of x must be...

   (A) Greater than 3
   (B) Greater than 6
   (C) Equal to 6
   (D) Equal to 3
   (E) Less than 3

IF YOU FINISH BEFORE TIME IS CALLED, YOU MAY CHECK YOUR WORK ON THIS SECTION ONLY. DO NOT TURN TO ANY OTHER SECTION IN THE TEST. | **STOP**

SSAT Middle Level Math Practice Test 2

2023 - 2023

Two Parts

Total number of questions: 50

Section 1: 25 questions

Section 2: 25 questions

Total time for two parts: 60 Minutes

SSAT Practice Test 2 Answer Sheet

Remove (or photocopy) this answer sheet and use it to complete the practice test.

SSAT Middle Level Mathematics Practice Test 2 Answer Sheet

SSAT Middle Level Practice Test 2 Section 1

#		#		#	
1	Ⓐ Ⓑ Ⓒ Ⓓ Ⓔ	11	Ⓐ Ⓑ Ⓒ Ⓓ Ⓔ	21	Ⓐ Ⓑ Ⓒ Ⓓ Ⓔ
2	Ⓐ Ⓑ Ⓒ Ⓓ Ⓔ	12	Ⓐ Ⓑ Ⓒ Ⓓ Ⓔ	22	Ⓐ Ⓑ Ⓒ Ⓓ Ⓔ
3	Ⓐ Ⓑ Ⓒ Ⓓ Ⓔ	13	Ⓐ Ⓑ Ⓒ Ⓓ Ⓔ	23	Ⓐ Ⓑ Ⓒ Ⓓ Ⓔ
4	Ⓐ Ⓑ Ⓒ Ⓓ Ⓔ	14	Ⓐ Ⓑ Ⓒ Ⓓ Ⓔ	24	Ⓐ Ⓑ Ⓒ Ⓓ Ⓔ
5	Ⓐ Ⓑ Ⓒ Ⓓ Ⓔ	15	Ⓐ Ⓑ Ⓒ Ⓓ Ⓔ	25	Ⓐ Ⓑ Ⓒ Ⓓ Ⓔ
6	Ⓐ Ⓑ Ⓒ Ⓓ Ⓔ	16	Ⓐ Ⓑ Ⓒ Ⓓ Ⓔ		
7	Ⓐ Ⓑ Ⓒ Ⓓ Ⓔ	17	Ⓐ Ⓑ Ⓒ Ⓓ Ⓔ		
8	Ⓐ Ⓑ Ⓒ Ⓓ Ⓔ	18	Ⓐ Ⓑ Ⓒ Ⓓ Ⓔ		
9	Ⓐ Ⓑ Ⓒ Ⓓ Ⓔ	19	Ⓐ Ⓑ Ⓒ Ⓓ Ⓔ		
10	Ⓐ Ⓑ Ⓒ Ⓓ Ⓔ	20	Ⓐ Ⓑ Ⓒ Ⓓ Ⓔ		

SSAT Middle Level Practice Test 2 Section 2

#		#		#	
1	Ⓐ Ⓑ Ⓒ Ⓓ Ⓔ	11	Ⓐ Ⓑ Ⓒ Ⓓ Ⓔ	21	Ⓐ Ⓑ Ⓒ Ⓓ Ⓔ
2	Ⓐ Ⓑ Ⓒ Ⓓ Ⓔ	12	Ⓐ Ⓑ Ⓒ Ⓓ Ⓔ	22	Ⓐ Ⓑ Ⓒ Ⓓ Ⓔ
3	Ⓐ Ⓑ Ⓒ Ⓓ Ⓔ	13	Ⓐ Ⓑ Ⓒ Ⓓ Ⓔ	23	Ⓐ Ⓑ Ⓒ Ⓓ Ⓔ
4	Ⓐ Ⓑ Ⓒ Ⓓ Ⓔ	14	Ⓐ Ⓑ Ⓒ Ⓓ Ⓔ	24	Ⓐ Ⓑ Ⓒ Ⓓ Ⓔ
5	Ⓐ Ⓑ Ⓒ Ⓓ Ⓔ	15	Ⓐ Ⓑ Ⓒ Ⓓ Ⓔ	25	Ⓐ Ⓑ Ⓒ Ⓓ Ⓔ
6	Ⓐ Ⓑ Ⓒ Ⓓ Ⓔ	16	Ⓐ Ⓑ Ⓒ Ⓓ Ⓔ		
7	Ⓐ Ⓑ Ⓒ Ⓓ Ⓔ	17	Ⓐ Ⓑ Ⓒ Ⓓ Ⓔ		
8	Ⓐ Ⓑ Ⓒ Ⓓ Ⓔ	18	Ⓐ Ⓑ Ⓒ Ⓓ Ⓔ		
9	Ⓐ Ⓑ Ⓒ Ⓓ Ⓔ	19	Ⓐ Ⓑ Ⓒ Ⓓ Ⓔ		
10	Ⓐ Ⓑ Ⓒ Ⓓ Ⓔ	20	Ⓐ Ⓑ Ⓒ Ⓓ Ⓔ		

SSAT Middle Level Math

Practice Test 2

Section 1

25 questions

Total time for this test: 30 Minutes

You may NOT use a calculator on this part.

1. How long does a 420–miles trip take moving at 65 miles per hour (*mph*)?
   (A) 4 *hours*
   (B) 6 *hours and* 24 *minutes*
   (C) 8 *hours and* 24 *minutes*
   (D) 8 *hours and* 30 *minutes*
   (E) 10 *hours and* 30 *minutes*

2. The marked price of a computer is D dollar. Its price decreased by 15% in January and later increased by 10% in February. What is the final price of the computer in D dollar?
   (A) 0.80 D
   (B) 0.88 D
   (C) 0.93 D
   (D) 1.20 D
   (E) 1.40 D

3. If 0.35 equals 350M, what is the value of M?
   (A) 0.001
   (B) 0.01
   (C) 1.0
   (D) 1.01
   (E) 1.001

4. Jason borrowed $5,800 for three months at an annual rate of 5%. How much interest did Jason owe?
   (A) $45
   (B) $72.50
   (C) $120
   (D) $240
   (E) $480

5. If three times a certain number, increased by 10, is equal to 40, what is the number?
   (A) 10
   (B) 12
   (C) 18
   (D) 27
   (E) 54

6. If 30 percent of a number is 150, then 15 percent of the same number is ?
   (A) 75
   (B) 79
   (C) 80
   (D) 90
   (E) 120

7. The average of $13, 15, 20$ and x is 20. What is the value of x?
   (A) 9
   (B) 15
   (C) 18
   (D) 20
   (E) 32

8. In five successive hours, a car traveled $40\ km, 45\ km, 50\ km, 35\ km$ and $55\ km$. In the next five hours, it traveled with an average speed of $55\ km\ per\ hour$. Find the total distance the car traveled in 10 hours.
   (A) $425\ km$
   (B) $450\ km$
   (C) $475\ km$
   (D) $500\ km$
   (E) $1,000\ km$

9. John has N toy cars. Jack has 6 more cars than John. If Jack gives John 3 cars, how many cars will Jack have, in terms of N?
   (A) N
   (B) $N - 1$
   (C) $N + 1$
   (D) $N + 2$
   (E) $N + 3$

10. What is the value of x in the following equation?

$$\frac{x + 4}{5} = 3$$

   (A) 2
   (B) 4
   (C) 6
   (D) 8
   (E) 11

11. The ratio of boys to girls in a school is $2:3$. If there are 500 students in a school, how many boys are in the school.
    (A) 540
    (B) 360
    (C) 300
    (D) 280
    (E) 200

12. Two third of 24 is equal to $\frac{2}{5}$ of what number?
    (A) 12
    (B) 20
    (C) 40
    (D) 60
    (E) 90

13. What is the cost of seven ounces of cheese at $0.96 *per pound*?
    (A) $0.42
    (B) $0.45
    (C) $0.48
    (D) $0.52
    (E) $0.64

14. If 60% of A is 30% of B, then B is what percent of A?
    (A) 3%
    (B) 30%
    (C) 200%
    (D) 300%
    (E) 900%

15. Sophia purchased a sofa for $504. The sofa is regularly priced at $600. What was the percent discount Sophia received on the sofa?
    (A) 12%
    (B) 16%
    (C) 20%
    (D) 25%
    (E) 40%

16. A bag contains 18 balls: two green, five black, eight blue, a brown, a red and one white. If 17 balls are removed from the bag at random, what is the probability that a brown ball has been removed?

(A) $\frac{1}{9}$

(B) $\frac{1}{18}$

(C) $\frac{16}{17}$

(D) $\frac{17}{18}$

(E) $\frac{1}{2}$

17. When a number is subtracted from 28 and the difference is divided by that number, the result is 3. What is the value of the number?
(A) 2
(B) 4
(C) 7
(D) 12
(E) 24

18. If 45% of a class are girls, and 25% of girls play tennis, approximately what percent of the class play tennis?
(A) 11%
(B) 15%
(C) 20%
(D) 40%
(E) 80%

19. 44 students took an exam and 11 of them failed. What percent of the students passed the exam?
(A) 20%
(B) 40%
(C) 60%
(D) 75%
(E) 90%

20. What is the value of x in the following equation?
$$3x + 10 = 67$$
(A) 5
(B) 7
(C) 9
(D) 11
(E) 19

21. If $N \times \frac{4}{3} \times 7 = 0$, then $N = \ldots$
(A) 0
(B) 1
(C) 2
(D) 3
(E) 4

22. Jason left a $12.00 tip on a lunch that cost $60.00, approximately what percentage was the tip?
(A) 2.5%
(B) 10%
(C) 15%
(D) 20%
(E) 25%

23. If 60% of a number is 6, what is the number?
(A) 4
(B) 8
(C) 10
(D) 12
(E) 20

24. If $\frac{z}{5} = 4$, then $z + 3 = ?$
(A) 4
(B) 5
(C) 15
(D) 20
(E) 23

25. In 1999, the average worker's income increased $3,000 per year starting from $24,000 annual salary. Which equation represents income greater than average? (I = income, x = number of years after 1999)

(A) $I > 3,000x + 24,000$

(B) $I > -3,000x + 24,000$

(C) $I < -3,000x + 24,000$

(D) $I < 3,000x - 24,000$

(E) $I < 24,000x + 24,000$

SSAT Middle Level Math

Practice Test 2

Section 2

25 questions

Total time for this test: 30 Minutes

You may NOT use a calculator on this part.

1. John has x dollars and he receives $150. He then buys a bicycle that costs
   $110. How much money does John have now?
   (A) $x + 150$
   (B) $x + 110$
   (C) $x + 40$
   (D) $x - 120$
   (E) $x - 40$

2. What is the value of x in this equation?
$$\frac{x - 3}{8} + 5 = 20$$

   (A) 131
   (B) 128
   (C) 123
   (D) 120
   (E) 115

3. Bob needs an 78% average in his writing class to pass. On his first 4 exams,
   he earned scores of 68%, 72%, 85%, and 90%. What is the minimum score
   Bob can earn on his fifth and final test to pass?
   (A) 80%,
   (B) 75%
   (C) 68%
   (D) 64%
   (E) 60%

4. The width of a rectangle is $6x$, the length is $8x$, and the perimeter is 84.
   What is the value of x?
   (A) 1
   (B) 2
   (C) 3
   (D) 4
   (E) 5

5. A bank is offering 3.5% simple interest on a savings account. If you deposit
   $8,000, how much interest will you earn in five years?
   (A) $360
   (B) $720
   (C) $1,400
   (D) $3,600
   (E) $4,800

6. If $(8 - 4) \times 4 = 8 + \square$, then $\square = ?$
   (A) 5
   (B) 6
   (C) 7
   (D) 8
   (E) 9

7. Jason is 9 miles ahead of Joe running at 6.5 miles per hour and Joe is running at the speed of 8 miles per hour. How long does it take Joe to catch Jason?
   (A) 3 *hours*
   (B) 4 *hours*
   (C) 6 *hours*
   (D) 8 *hours*
   (E) 10 *hours*

8. In a classroom, there are y tables that can each seat 4 people and there are x tables that can each seat 8 people. What is the number of people that can be seated in the classroom?
   (A) $4y$
   (B) $8x$
   (C) $8x - 4y$
   (D) 13
   (E) $8x + 4y$

9. The area of a circle is 81π. What is the diameter of the circle?
   (A) 4
   (B) 8
   (C) 12
   (D) 14
   (E) 18

10. A shirt costing $300 is discounted 15%. After a month, the shirt is discounted another 15%. Which of the following expressions can be used to find the selling price of the shirt?
    (A) $(300)(0.70)$
    (B) $(300) - 300(0.30)$
    (C) $(300)(0.15) - (300)(0.15)$
    (D) $(300)(0.85)(0.85)$
    (E) $(300)(0.85)(0.85) - (300)(0.15)$

11. Four one – foot rulers can be split among how many users to leave each with $\frac{1}{3}$ of a ruler?
   (A) 4
   (B) 6
   (C) 12
   (D) 24
   (E) 48

12. The perimeter of a rectangular yard is 72 meters. What is its length if its width is twice its length?
   (A) 12 *meters*
   (B) 18 *meters*
   (C) 20 *meters*
   (D) 24 *meters*
   (E) 36 *meters*

13. What is the value of x in this equation? $2x + 10 = 48$
   (A) 19
   (B) 14
   (C) 12
   (D) 10
   (E) 6

14. The mean of 50 test scores was calculated as 86. But, it turned out that one of the scores was misread as 94 but it was 69. What is the mean?
   (A) 85.5
   (B) 85
   (C) 84.5
   (D) 83.5
   (E) 80.5

15. The average of 6 numbers is 15. The average of 4 of those numbers is 10. What is the average of the other two numbers?
   (A) 10
   (B) 12
   (C) 14
   (D) 15
   (E) 25

16. If $x + 5 = 8$, $2y - 1 = 5$ then $xy + 15 =$
   (A) 10
   (B) 19
   (C) 24
   (D) 27
   (E) 32

17. A card is drawn at random from a standard 52–card deck, what is the probability that the card is of Hearts? (The deck includes 13 of each suit clubs, diamonds, hearts, and spades)
   (A) $\frac{1}{3}$
   (B) $\frac{1}{4}$
   (C) $\frac{1}{6}$
   (D) $\frac{1}{52}$
   (E) $\frac{1}{104}$

18. Which of the following is NOT less than $\frac{1}{5}$?
   (A) $\frac{1}{8}$
   (B) $\frac{1}{3}$
   (C) $\frac{1}{9}$
   (D) 0.14
   (E) 17%

19. Mr. Jones saves \$2,500 out of his monthly family income of \$65,000. What fractional part of his income does he save?
   (A) $\frac{1}{26}$
   (B) $\frac{1}{11}$
   (C) $\frac{3}{25}$
   (D) $\frac{2}{15}$
   (E) $\frac{1}{15}$

20. If $5x - 6 = 39$, then $3x + 6 =$?
   (A) 18
   (B) 20
   (C) 22
   (D) 33
   (E) 36

21. In two successive years, the population of a town is increased by 10% and 20%. What percent of the population is increased after two years?
(A) 32%
(B) 31%
(C) 30%
(D) 28%
(E) 22%

22. If 150% of a number is 75, then what is the 80% of that number?
(A) 40
(B) 50
(C) 70
(D) 85
(E) 90

23. What is the equivalent temperature of 140°F in Celsius? (C = Celsius)

$$C = \frac{5}{9}(F - 32)$$

(A) 32
(B) 40
(C) 48
(D) 52
(E) 60

24. The perimeter of the trapezoid below (not drawn to scale) is 38 cm. What is its area?

(A) 48 cm^2
(B) 78 cm^2
(C) 168 cm^2
(D) 576 cm^2
(E) 986 cm^2

25. The width of a box is one third of its length. The height of the box is half of its width. If the length of the box is 24 cm, what is the volume of the box?
   (A) 81 cm^3
   (B) 162 cm^3
   (C) 243 cm^3
   (D) 768 cm^3
   (E) 1880 cm^3

IF YOU FINISH BEFORE TIME IS CALLED, YOU MAY CHECK YOUR WORK ON THIS SECTION ONLY. DO NOT TURN TO ANY OTHER SECTION IN THE TEST.   STOP

SSAT Middle Level Practice Tests Answer Keys

Now, it's time to review your results to see where you went wrong and what areas you need to improve!

SSAT Middle Level Math Practice Test 1								SSAT Middle Level Math Practice Test 2							
Section 1				Section 2				Section 1				Section 2			
1	E	16	A	1	D	16	C	1	B	16	D	1	C	16	C
2	D	17	A	2	C	17	B	2	C	17	C	2	C	17	B
3	C	18	C	3	E	18	D	3	A	18	A	3	B	18	B
4	E	19	C	4	C	19	E	4	B	19	D	4	C	19	A
5	D	20	D	5	A	20	C	5	A	20	E	5	C	20	D
6	B	21	D	6	E	21	E	6	A	21	A	6	D	21	A
7	B	22	B	7	B	22	B	7	E	22	D	7	C	22	A
8	B	23	D	8	C	23	B	8	D	23	C	8	E	23	E
9	B	24	A	9	D	24	C	9	E	24	E	9	E	24	B
10	D	25	D	10	C	25	B	10	E	25	A	10	D	25	D
11	A			11	B			11	E			11	C		
12	C			12	E			12	C			12	A		
13	D			13	C			13	A			13	A		
14	C			14	D			14	C			14	A		
15	B			15	A			15	B			15	E		

Score Your Test

SSAT scores are broken down by its three sections: Verbal, Mathematics, and Reading. A sum of the three sections is also reported.

For the Middle Level SSAT, the score range is 500-800, the lowest possible score a student can earn is 500 and the highest score is 800 for each section. A student receives 1 point for every correct answer and loses $\frac{1}{4}$ point for each incorrect answer. No points are lost by skipping a question.

The total scaled score for a Middle Level SSAT test is the sum of the scores for the Mathematics, verbal, and reading sections. A student will also receive a percentile score of between 1-99% that compares that student's test scores with those of other test takers of same grade and gender from the past 3 years.

Use the following table to convert SSAT Middle level raw score to scaled score.

SSAT Middle Level Math Scaled Scores	
Raw Scores	Mathematics
50	710
45	680
40	660
35	635
30	615
25	590
20	570
15	540
10	525
5	500
0	480
-5	460
- 10 and lower	440

SSAT Middle Level Practice Tests Answers and Explanations

SSAT Middle Level Mathematics Practice Test 1 Section 1

1) Choice E is correct

If 30 percent of a number is 60, then the number is: $30\% \ of \ x = 60 \rightarrow 0.3x = 60 \rightarrow$
$x = \frac{60}{0.3} = \frac{600}{3} = 200$, 20 percent of 200 is: $20\% \ of \ 200 = \frac{20}{100} \times 200 = 40$

2) Choice D is correct

$2 \times 0.4 = 0.8$, all **choices** provided are equal to 0.8 except option D. $\frac{5}{15} \times 3 = 1$

3) Choice C is correct

Sara has M books. Mary has 6 more books than Sara. Then, Mary has $M + 6$
books. If Mary gives Sara 4 books, Mary will have: $M + 6 - 4 = M + 2$

4) Choice E is correct

If $\frac{x}{2} = 30$, then $\frac{3x}{2}$ is 3 times $\frac{x}{2}$. The answer is 90.

5) Choice D is correct

$\frac{1}{6}$ of 40 is 6.66. Let's review the **choices** provided:

(A) $0.3 \times 6 = 1.8$
(B) $0.3 \times 5 = 1.5$
(C) $0.2 \times 30 = 6$
(D) $0.2 \times 35 = 7$
(E) $0.2 \times 39.5 = 7.9$

Option D is the closest to 6.66

6) Choice B is correct

The diagonal of the square is 8. Let x be the side.

Use Pythagorean Theorem: $a^2 + b^2 = c^2$

$x^2 + x^2 = 8^2 \Rightarrow 2x^2 = 8^2 \Rightarrow 2x^2 = 64 \Rightarrow x^2 = 32 \Rightarrow x = \sqrt{32}$

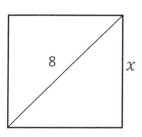

The area of the square is: $\sqrt{32} \times \sqrt{32} = 32$

7) Choice B is correct

The sum of supplement angles is 180. Let x be that angle. Therefore, $x + 5x = 180$

$6x = 180$, divide both sides by 6: $x = 30$

8) Choice B is correct

Use the formula for Percent of Change: $\dfrac{\text{New Value} - \text{Old Value}}{Old\ Value} \times 100\%$

$\dfrac{28-44}{44} \times 100\% \approx -36\%$ (negative sign here means that the new price is less than old price)

9) Choice B is correct

$One\ liter = 1{,}000\ cm^3 \rightarrow 6\ liters = 6{,}000 cm^3$, $6{,}000 = 25 \times 5 \times h \rightarrow h = \dfrac{6{,}000}{125} = 48\ cm$

10) Choice D is correct

The perimeter of the trapezoid is 56.

Therefore, the missing side is $= 56 - 17 - 16 - 8 = 15$

Area of a trapezoid: $A = \dfrac{1}{2}h(b_1 + b_2) = \dfrac{1}{2}(15)(8 + 16) = \dfrac{1}{2}(15)(24) = 180$

11) Choice A is correct

If the score of Mia was 40, therefore the score of Ava is 20. Since, the score of Emma was half as that of Ava, therefore, the score of Emma is 10.

12) Choice C is correct

Let x be the number. Write the equation and solve for x. $\dfrac{2}{3} \times 9 = \dfrac{2}{5} . x \Rightarrow \dfrac{2 \times 9}{3} = \dfrac{2x}{5}$, use cross multiplication to solve for x. $5 \times 18 = 2x \times 3 \Rightarrow 90 = 6x \Rightarrow x = 15$

13) Choice D is correct

Let x be the number. Then: $3x + 5 = 32$ Solve for x: $3x + 5 = 32 \rightarrow 3x = 32 - 5 = 27 \rightarrow x = 27 \div 3 = 9$

14) Choice C is correct

Simplify and solve for x in the equation. $4(x + 1) = 6(x - 4) + 20$, $4x + 4 = 6x - 24 + 20$, $4x + 4 = 6x - 4$. Subtract $4x$ from both sides: $4 = 2x - 4$, Add 4 to both sides: $8 = 2x$, $4 = x$

15) Choice B is correct

Let's write equations based on the information provided:

$Michelle = Karen - 9, Michelle = David - 4,\ Karen + Michelle + David = 82$

$Karen - 9 = Michelle \Rightarrow Karen = Michelle + 9$

$Karen + Michelle + David = 82$

Now, replace the ages of Karen and David by Michelle. Then:

$Michelle + 9 + Michelle + Michelle + 4 = 82$

$3 \times Michelle + 13 = 82 \Rightarrow 3 \times Michelle = 82 - 13$

$3 \times Michelle = 69$, $Michelle = 23$

16) Choice A is correct

Let x be one-kilogram orange cost, then: $2x + (2 \times 4.2) = 26.4 \rightarrow 2x + 8.4 = 26.4 \rightarrow 2x = 26.4 - 8.4 \rightarrow 2x = 18 \rightarrow x = \frac{18}{2} = \$9$

17) Choice A is correct

$average = \frac{sum\ of\ terms}{number\ of\ terms}$, The sum of the weight of all girls is: $18 \times 50 = 900kg$, The sum of the weight of all boys is: $32 \times 62 = 1,984\ kg$, The sum of the weight of all students is:

$900 + 1,984 = 2,884\ kg$, $Average = \frac{2,884}{50} = 57.68$

18) Choice C is correct

Solve for x in the equation. $6(x + 4) = 78 \rightarrow 6x + 24 = 78 \rightarrow 6x = 78 - 24 = 54 \rightarrow x = 54 \div 6 = 9$

19) Choice C is correct

Let x be the number. Write the equation and solve for x. $(32 - x) \div x = 3$
Multiply both sides by x. $(32 - x) = 3x$, then add x both sides. $32 = 4x$, now divide both sides by 4. $x = 8$

20) Choice D is correct

Only option D is correct. $\frac{5}{6} = 0.83 \rightarrow 0.8 < \frac{5}{6}$

21) Choice D is correct

In a group of 5 books, the average number of pages is 24. Therefore, the sum of pages in all 5 books is $(5 \times 24 = 120)$. Mary adds a book with 36 pages to the group. Then, the sum of pages in all 6 books is $(5 \times 24 + 36 = 156)$. The new average number of pages per book is: $\frac{156}{6} = 26$

22) Choice B is correct

Choices A, C, D, and E are incorrect because 70% of each of the numbers is a non-whole number.

A. 49, $70\%\ of\ 49\ =\ 0.70 \times 49 = 34.3$
B. 40, $70\%\ of\ 40 = 0.70 \times 40 = 28$
C. 32, $70\%\ of\ 32 = 0.80 \times 32 = 22.4$
D. 12, $70\%\ of\ 12 = 0.70 \times 12 = 8.4$
E. 9, $70\%\ of\ 9 = 0.80 \times 9 = 6.3$

23) Choice D is correct

$$\frac{2}{5} \times 35 = \frac{70}{5} = 14$$

24) Choice A is correct

$$x = 25 + 125 = 150$$

25) Choice D is correct

The red box is 20% bigger than the blue box. Let x be the capacity of the blue box. Then:

$$x + 20\%\ of\ x = 36 \rightarrow 1.2x = 36 \rightarrow x = \frac{36}{1.2} = 30$$

SSAT Middle Level Mathematics Practice Test 1 Section 2

1) Choice D is correct

$8 \times 10 = \$80$, Petrol use: $10 \times 2 = 20$ liters, Petrol cost: $20 \times \$1 = \$20$

Money earned: $\$80 - \$20 = \$60$

2) Choice C is correct

From the **choices** provided, only C $(\frac{1}{7})$ is less than $\frac{1}{5}$.

3) Choice E is correct

Amy earns $\$30.00$ *per hour* now. $\$30.00$ *per hour* is 20 percent more than her previous rate. Let x be her rate before her raise. Then: $x + 0.20x = 30 \to 1.2x = 30 \to x = \frac{30}{1.2} = 25$

John earns $\$28.80$ *per hour* now. $\$28.80$ *per hour* is 20 percent more than his previous rate. Let x be John's rate before his raise. Then: $x + 0.20x = 28.80 \to 1.2x = 28.80 \to x = \frac{28.80}{1.2} = 24$, Amy earned $\$1.00$ more per hour than John before their raises.

4) Choice C is correct.

Three people can paint 3 houses in 12 days. It means that for painting 6 houses in 12 days we need 6 people. To paint 6 houses in 6 days, 12 people are needed.

5) Choice A is correct.

$N \times (6 - 3) = 12 \to N \times 3 = 12 \to N = 4$

6) Choice E is correct.

The length of the rectangle is 24. Then, its width is 8. $24 \div 3 = 8$

$\textit{Perimeter of a rectangle} = 2 \times \textit{width} + 2 \times \textit{length} = 2 \times 8 + 2 \times 24 = 16 + 48 = 64$

7) Choice B is correct

Let write angles A and B in the figure. $A = 180° - 112° = 68°$, $B = 180° - 145° = 40°$

The sum of all angles in a triangle is 180 degrees. Then: $x + A + B = 180° \to$

$$x = 180° - 68° - 40° = 72°$$

8) Choice C is correct.

If $x \blacksquare y = 4x + y - 2$, Then: $4 \blacksquare 12 = 4(4) + 12 - 2 = 16 + 12 - 2 = 26$

9) Choice D is correct

The width of a rectangle is $4x$ and its length is $6x$. Therefore, the perimeter of the rectangle is $20x$. *Perimeter of a rectangle* $= 2(width + length) = 2(4x + 6x) = 2(10x) = 20x$

The perimeter of the rectangle is 90. Then: $20x = 90 \rightarrow x = 4.5$

10) Choice C is correct

The area of the floor is: $7\ cm \times 24\ cm = 168\ cm^2$, The number is tiles needed $= 168 \div 8 = 21$

11) Choice B is correct

0.65 equals $65M$. Then: $65M = 0.65 \rightarrow M = \frac{0.65}{65} = 0.01$

12) Choice E is correct

$z = 3x + 5$, then, $2z = 2(3x + 5) = 6x + 10$, $2z + 3 = 6x + 10 + 3 = 6x + 13$

13) Choice C is correct.

$96 = 8x \times 4 \rightarrow x = 96 \div 4 = 24 \rightarrow x = 3$
x equals to 3. Let's review the choices provided:
A) $x + 4 \rightarrow 3 + 4 = 7$ 96 is not divisible by 9.
B) $2x - 4 \rightarrow 2 \times 3 - 1 = 5$ 96 is not divisible by 5.
C) $5x - 3 \rightarrow 5 \times 3 - 3 = 12$ 96 is divisible by 12.
D) $x \times 3 \rightarrow 3 \times 3 = 9$ 96 is not divisible by 9.
E) $3x + 1 \rightarrow 3 \times 3 + 1 = 10$ 96 is not divisible by 10.

The answer is C.

14) Choice D is correct

$\frac{1}{16} = 0.0625 \rightarrow C = 5, \frac{1}{25} = 0.04 \rightarrow D = 4 \rightarrow C \times D = 5 \times 4 = 20$

15) Choice A is correct

Use cross product to solve for x.

$\frac{x}{x-2} = \frac{4}{5} \rightarrow 5 \times x = 4 \times (x - 2) \rightarrow 5x = 4x - 8 \rightarrow x = -8, x - 5 = -8 - 5 = -13$

16) Choice C is correct

x is the number of all sales profit and 3% of it is: $3\% \times x = 0.03x$, Employer's revenue: $0.03x + 7,000$

17) Choice B is correct

Number of biology book: 35, Total number of books; $35 + 85 + 90 = 210$

The ratio of the number of biology books to the total number of books is: $\frac{35}{210} = \frac{1}{6}$

18) Choice D is correct.

$5,000 + A - 200 = 7,400 \to 5,000 + A = 7,400 + 200 = 7,600 \to A = 7,600 - 5,000 = 2,600$

19) Choice E is correct

Let x be all expenses, then $\frac{22}{100}x = \$770 \to x = \frac{100 \times \$770}{22} = \$3,500$,

He spent for his rent: $\frac{27}{100} \times \$3,500 = \$945$

20) Choice C is correct

$5 \times M + 3 = 5 \to 5 \times M = 5 - 3 = 2 \to M = \frac{2}{5}$

21) Choice E is correct

$\frac{52.6}{100} = 0.526$

22) Choice B is correct

The angles on a straight line add up to 180 degrees. Then: $x + 22 + y + 2x + y = 180$, Then, $3x + 2y = 180 - 22 \to 3(28) + 2y = 158 \to 2y = 158 - 84 = 74 \to y = 37$

23) Choice B is correct

let x be the number of gallons of water the container holds when it is full.

Then; $\frac{5}{24}x = 2.5 \to x = \frac{24 \times 2.5}{5} = 12$

24) Choice C is correct.

The ratio of lions to tigers is 3 to 1 at the zoo. Therefore, total number of lions and tigers must be divisible by 4. From the choices provided, only 98 is not divisible by 4.

25) Choice B is correct

If x is greater than 18, then $\frac{1}{3}$ of x must be greater than: $\frac{1}{3} \times 18 = 6$.

SSAT Middle Level Mathematics Practice Test 2 Section 1

1) Choice B is correct

Use distance formula: $Distance = Rate \times time \Rightarrow 420 = 65 \times T$, divide both sides by 65. $420 \div 65 = T \Rightarrow T = 6.4\ hours$. Change hours to minutes for the decimal part. $0.4\ hours = 0.4 \times 60 = 24\ minutes$.

2) Choice C is correct

To find the discount, multiply the number by $(100\% - rate\ of\ discount)$. Therefore, for the first discount we get: $(D)\ (100\% - 15\%) = (D)\ (0.85) = 0.85\ D$

For increase of 10%: $(0.85\ D)\ (100\% + 10\%) = (0.85\ D)\ (1.10) = 0.93\ D = 93\%\ of\ D\ or\ 0.93D$

3) Choice A is correct

0.35 equals $350M$. Then: $0.35 = 350M \rightarrow M = \frac{0.35}{350} = 0.001$

4) Choice B is correct

Use simple interest formula: $I = prt$, (I = interest, p = principal, r = rate, t = time)

t is for one year. For 3 months, t is $\frac{1}{4}$ or 0.25. $I = (5,800)(0.05)(0.25) = 72.50$

5) Choice A is correct

Three times a certain number, increased by 10, is equal to 40. Write an equation and solve.

$3x + 10 = 40 \rightarrow 3x = 40 - 10 = 30 \rightarrow x = \dfrac{30}{3} = 10$

6) Choice A is correct

30 percent of a number is 150. Therefore, the number is 500. $0.30x = 150 \rightarrow x = \dfrac{150}{0.30} = 500$

15 percent of 500 is 75. $0.15 \times 500 = 75$

7) Choice E is correct

$$average = \frac{sum\ of\ terms}{number\ of\ terms} \Rightarrow 20 = \frac{13 + 15 + 20 + x}{4} \Rightarrow 80 = 48 + x \Rightarrow x = 32$$

8) Choice D is correct

Add the first 5 numbers. $40 + 45 + 50 + 35 + 55 = 225$

To find the distance traveled in the next 5 hours, multiply the average by number of hours.

Distance = Average × Rate = $55 \times 5 = 275$, Add both numbers. $275 + 225 = 500$

9) Choice E is correct

John has N toy cars. Jack has 6 more cars than John. Therefore, Jack has $N + 6$ toy cars. Jack gives John 3 cars. Now, Jack has $(N + 6 - 3)$ $N + 3$ toy cars.

10) Choice E is correct

$\frac{x + 4}{5} = 3 \rightarrow x + 4 = 3 \times 5 = 15 \rightarrow x = 15 - 4 = 11$

11) Choice E is correct

Th ratio of boy to girls is $2:3$. Therefore, there are 2 boys out of 5 students. To find the answer, first divide the total number of students by 5, then multiply the result by 2.

$500 \div 5 = 100 \Rightarrow 100 \times 2 = 200$

12) Choice C is correct

Let x be the number. Write the equation and solve for x. $\frac{2}{3} \times 24 = \frac{2}{5} . x \Rightarrow$ $\frac{2 \times 24}{3} = \frac{2x}{5}$, use cross multiplication to solve for x. $5 \times 48 = 2x \times 3 \Rightarrow 240 = 6x \Rightarrow$ $x = 40$

13) Choice A is correct

One pound of cheese costs $\$0.96$. *One pound* = 16 *ounces*, 16 ounces of cheese costs $\$0.96$. Then, 1 ounce of chees costs $(0.96 \div 16)$ $\$0.06$. 7 ounces of cheese costs $(7 \times \$0.06)$ $\$0.42$.

14) Choice C is correct

Write the equation and solve for B: $0.60A = 0.30B$, divide both sides by 0.30, then you will have $\frac{0.60}{0.30} A = B$, therefore: $B = 2A$, and B is 2 times of A or it's 200% of A.

15) Choice B is correct

$\frac{504}{600} = 0.84$. 504 is 84 percent of 600. So, the discount is 16%. $100\% - 16\% = 84\%$

16) Choice D is correct

If 17 balls are removed from the bag at random, there will be one ball in the bag. The probability of choosing a brown ball is 1 out of 18. Therefore, the probability of not choosing a brown ball is 17 out of 18 and the probability of having not a brown ball after removing 17 balls is the same.

17) Choice C is correct

Let x be the number. Write the equation and solve for x. $(28 - x) \div x = 3$. Multiply both sides by x. $(28 - x) = 3x$, then add x both sides. $28 = 4x$, now divide both sides by 4. $x = 7$

18) Choice A is correct

The percent of girls playing tennis is: $45\% \times 25\% = 0.45 \times 0.25 \approx 0.11 = 11\%$

19) Choice D is correct

The failing rate is 11 out of $44 = \frac{11}{55}$. Change the fraction to percent:
$\frac{11}{44} \times 100\% = 25\%$

25 percent of students failed. Therefore, 75 percent of students passed the exam.

20) Choice E is correct

$3x + 10 = 67 \rightarrow 3x = 67 - 10 = 57 \rightarrow x = \dfrac{57}{3} = 19$

21) Choice A is correct

$N \times \frac{4}{3} \times 7 = 0$, then N must be 0.

22) Choice D is correct

\$12 is what percent of \$60? $12 \div 60 = 0.20 = 20\%$

23) Choice C is correct

Let x be the number. Write the equation and solve for x.

60% *of* $x = 6 \Rightarrow 0.60 \, x = 6 \Rightarrow x = 6 \div 0.60 = 10$

24) Choice E is correct

$\frac{z}{5} = 4 \rightarrow z = 4 \times 5 = 20, z + 3 = 20 + 3 = 23$

25) Choice A is correct

Let x be the number of years. Therefore, \$3,000 per year equals $3000x$. starting from \$24,000 annual salary means you should add that amount to $2000x$. Income more than that is:

$I > 3000x + 24000$

SSAT Middle Level Mathematics Practice Test 2 Section 2

1) Choice C is correct

John has x dollars and he receives $150. Therefore, he has $x + 150$.

He then buys a bicycle that costs $110. Now, he has: $x + 150 - 110 = x + 40$

2) Choice C is correct

$$\frac{x-3}{8} + 5 = 20 \rightarrow \frac{x-3}{8} = 20 - 5 = 15 \rightarrow x - 3 = 15 \times 8 = 120 \rightarrow$$
$$x = 120 + 3 = 123$$

3) Choice B is correct

Bob needs an 78% average to pass for five exams. Therefore, the sum of 5 exams must be at lease $5 \times 78 = 390$, The sum of 4 exams is: $68 + 72 + 85 + 90 = 315$.

The minimum score Bob can earn on his fifth and final test to pass is: $390 - 315 = 75$

4) Choice C is correct

The width of a rectangle is $6x$ and its length is $8x$. Then, the perimeter of the rectangle is $28x$.

Perimeter of a rectangle $= 2(width + length) = 2(6x + 8x) = 28x$

The perimeter of the rectangle is 84. Then: $28x = 84 \rightarrow x = 3$

5) Choice C is correct

Use simple interest formula: $I = prt$, (I = interest, p = principal, r = rate, t = time)

$I = (8,000)(0.035)(5) = 1,400$

6) Choice D is correct

$(8 - 4) \times 4 = 8 + \square$

Then: $4 \times 4 = 8 + \square$, $16 = 8 + \square$, then $\square = 8$

7) Choice C is correct

The distance between Jason and Joe is 9 miles. Jason running at 6.5 miles per hour and Joe is running at the speed of 8 miles per hour. Therefore, every hour the distance is 1.5 miles less.

$9 \div 1.5 = 6$

8) Choice E is correct

There are y tables that can each seat 4 people and there are x tables that can each seat 8 people. Therefore, $4y + 8x$ people can be seated in the classroom

9) Choice E is correct

The formula for the area of the circle is: $A = \pi r^2$

The area of the circle is 81π. Therefore: $A = \pi r^2 \Rightarrow 81\pi = \pi r^2$, Divide both sides by π: $81 = r^2 \Rightarrow r = 9$, Diameter of a circle is $2 \times$ radius. Then: Diameter $= 2 \times 9 = 18$

10) Choice D is correct

To find the discount, multiply the number by $(100\% - rate\ of\ discount)$. Therefore, for the first discount we get: $(300)(100\% - 15\%) = (300)(0.85)$, For the next 15% discount: $(300)(0.85)(0.85)$

11) Choice C is correct

$4 \div \dfrac{1}{3} = 12$

12) Choice A is correct

The width of the rectangle is twice its length. Let x be the length. Then, $width = 2x$

Perimeter of the rectangle is $2\ (width + length) = 2(2x + x) = 72 \Rightarrow 6x = 72 \Rightarrow x = 12$

Length of the rectangle is 12 meters.

13) Choice A is correct

$2x + 10 = 48 \rightarrow 2x = 48 - 10 = 38 \rightarrow x = \dfrac{38}{2} = 19$

14) Choice A is correct

$average\ (mean) = \dfrac{sum\ of\ terms}{number\ of\ terms} \Rightarrow 86 = \dfrac{sum\ of\ terms}{50} \Rightarrow sum = 86 \times 50 = 4300$

The difference of 94 and 69 is 25. Therefore, 25 should be subtracted from the sum.

$4300 - 25 = 4275$, $mean = \dfrac{sum\ of\ terms}{number\ of\ terms} \Rightarrow mean = \dfrac{4275}{50} = 85.5$

15) Choice E is correct

$average = \frac{sum\ of\ terms}{number\ of\ terms} \Rightarrow$ (average of 6 numbers) $15 = \frac{sum\ of\ numbers}{6} \Rightarrow$ sum of 6 numbers is $15 \times 6 = 90$

(average of 4 numbers) $10 = \frac{sum\ of\ numbers}{4} \Rightarrow$ sum of 4 numbers is $10 \times 4 = 40$

$sum\ of\ 6\ numbers - sum\ of\ 4\ numbers = sum\ of\ 2\ numbers$

$90 - 40 = 50$ average of 2 numbers $= \frac{50}{2} = 25$

16) Choice C is correct

$x + 5 = 8 \rightarrow x = 8 - 5 = 3, 2y - 1 = 5 \rightarrow 2y = 6 \rightarrow y = 3, xy + 15 = 3 \times 3 + 15 = 24$

17) Choice B is correct

The probability of choosing a Hearts is $\frac{13}{52} = \frac{1}{4}$

18) Choice B is correct

From the choices provided, only $\frac{1}{3}$ is greater than $\frac{1}{5}$.

19) Choice A is correct

2,500 out of 65,000 equals to $\frac{2500}{65000} = \frac{25}{650} = \frac{1}{26}$

20) Choice D is correct

$5x - 6 = 39 \rightarrow 5x = 39 + 6 = 45 \rightarrow x = 9$, then $3x + 6 = 3 \times 9 + 6 = 27 + 6 = 33$

21) Choice A is correct

the population is increased by 10% and 20%. 10% increase changes the population to 110% of original population. For the second increase, multiply the result by 120%.

$(1.10) \times (1.20) = 1.32 = 132\%$, 32 percent of the population is increased after two years.

22) Choice A is correct

First, find the number. Let x be the number. Write the equation and solve for x.

150% of a number is 75, then: $1.5 \times x = 75 \Rightarrow x = 75 \div 1.5 = 50$. 80% of 50 is: $0.8 \times 50 = 40$

23) Choice E is correct

Plug in 104 for F and then solve for C.

$$C = \frac{5}{9}(F - 32) \Rightarrow C = \frac{5}{9}(140 - 32) \Rightarrow C = \frac{5}{9}(108) = 60$$

24) Choice B is correct

The perimeter of the trapezoid is 38 cm. Therefore, the missing side is:

$38 - 13 - 9 - 4 = 12$. Area of a trapezoid: $A = \frac{1}{2}h(b_1 + b_2) = \frac{1}{2}(12)(4 + 9) = 78$

25) Choice D is correct

If the length of the box is 24, then the width of the box is one third of it, 8, and the height of the box is 4 (half of the width). The volume of the box is:

$Volume\ of\ a\ box = (length) \times (width) \times (height) = (24) \times (8) \times (4) = 768$

... So Much More Online!

Effortless Math Online SSAT Middle Level Center offers a complete study program, including the following:

- ✓ Step-by-step instructions on how to prepare for the SSAT Middle Level test

- ✓ Numerous SSAT Middle Level worksheets to help you measure your math skills

- ✓ Complete list of SSAT formulas

- ✓ Video lessons for SSAT topics

- ✓ Full-length SSAT practice tests

- ✓ And much more...

No Registration Required.

Receive the PDF version of this book or get another FREE book!

Thank you for using our Book!

Do you LOVE this book?

Then, you can get the PDF version of this book or another book absolutely FREE!

Please email us at:

info@EffortlessMath.com

for details.

Author's Final Note

I hope you enjoyed reading this book. You've made it through the book! Great job!

First of all, thank you for purchasing this study guide. I know you could have picked any number of books to help you prepare for your SSAT Middle Level test, but you picked this book and for that I am extremely grateful.

It took me years to write this workbook for the SSAT Middle Level because I wanted to prepare a comprehensive SSAT Middle Level prep book to help test takers make the most effective use of their valuable time while preparing for the test.

After teaching and tutoring math courses for over a decade, I've gathered my personal notes and lessons to develop this study guide. It is my greatest hope that the lessons in this book could help you prepare for your test successfully.

If you have any questions, please contact me at reza@effortlessmath.com and I will be glad to assist. Your feedback will help me to greatly improve the quality of my books in the future and make this book even better. Furthermore, I expect that I have made a few minor errors somewhere in this book. If you think this to be the case, please let me know so I can fix the issue as soon as possible.

If you enjoyed this book and found some benefit in reading this, I'd like to hear from you and hope that you could take a quick minute to post a review on the book's Amazon page. To leave your valuable feedback, please visit: amzn.to/36sx27M

Or scan this QR code.

I personally go over every single review, to make sure my books really are reaching out and helping students and test takers. Please help me help SSAT Middle Level test takers, by leaving a review!

I wish you all the best in your future success!

Reza Nazari

Math teacher and author

Made in United States
Orlando, FL
17 October 2023

37960677R00098